THE
HIDDEN FORCES
OF
LIFE

Selections from the Works of
SRI AUROBINDO
and
THE MOTHER

Compiled by
A. S. Dalal

INSTITUTE OF INTEGRAL PSYCHOLOGY
OJAI, CALIFORNIA

First Edition 1990
Reprinted 1994

Published in the United States by Institute of Integral Psychology, Ojai, California, and simultaneously in India by Sri Aurobindo Ashram, Publication.Department, Pondicherry, India.

Distributed in the United States by
Lotus Light Publications
P.O. Box 325
Twin Lakes, W1 53181

ISBN 0-941524-60-4

Library of Congress Catalog Card Number 89-51865

Printed at Sri Aurobindo Ashram Press, Pondicherry
PRINTED IN INDIA

The compiler is grateful to Lloyd W. Fellows, Ph.D., Founder-Director of the Institute of Integral Psychology for sponsoring the publication of this book in the United States, and to Sri Aurobindo Ashram, Copyright Department, for permission to bring out an American edition of the book.

All that transpires on earth and all beyond
Are parts of an illimitable plan
The One keeps in his heart and knows alone.
Our outward happenings have their seed within,
And even this random Fate that imitates Chance,
This mass of unintelligible results,
Are the dumb graph of truths that work unseen:
The laws of the Unknown create the known.
The events that shape the appearance of our lives
Are a cipher of subliminal quiverings
Which rarely we surprise or vaguely feel,
Are an outcome of suppressed realities
That hardly rise into material day:
They are born from the spirit's sun of hidden powers
Digging a tunnel through emergency.
But who shall pierce into the cryptic gulf
And learn what deep necessity of the soul
Determined casual deed and consequence?
Absorbed in a routine of daily acts,
Our eyes are fixed on an external scene;
We hear the crash of the wheels of Circumstance
And wonder at the hidden cause of things.

SRI AUROBINDO
Savitri, Book One, Canto Four

Our conscious movements have sealed origins
But with those shadowy seats no converse hold;
No understanding binds our comrade parts;
Our acts emerge from a crypt our minds ignore.
Our deepest depths are ignorant of themselves;
Even our body is a mystery shop;
As our earth's roots lurk screened below our earth,
So lie unseen our roots of mind and life.
Our springs are kept close hid beneath, within;
Our souls are moved by powers behind the wall.
In the subterranean reaches of the spirit
A puissance acts and recks not what it means;
Using unthinking monitors and scribes,
It is the cause of what we think and feel.
The troglodytes of the subconscious Mind,
Ill-trained slow stammering interpreters,
Only of their small task's routine aware
And busy with the record in our cells,
Concealed in the subliminal secrecies
Mid an obscure occult machinery,
Capture the mystic Morse whose measured lilt
Transmits the messages of the cosmic Force.
A whisper falls into life's inner ear
And echoes from the dun subconscient caves,
Speech leaps, thought quivers, the heart vibrates, the will
Answers and tissue and nerve obey the call.
Our lives translate these subtle intimacies;
All is the commerce of a secret Power.

SRI AUROBINDO
Savitri, Book Two, Canto Five

CONTENTS

PREFACE

A retrospective review of the course of one's life is apt to reveal that whereas some events in the past were the outcome of one's conscious choice and deliberate effort, a good number of incidents, including perhaps some of the most significant happenings that have determined the course of one's life, were unplanned and unforeseen. It is in what are regarded as the major events and milestones of one's life – such as choosing a course of studies or training after high school, selecting a career, decisions pertaining to marriage, living in a particular city or country, and the like – that personal choice and will are usually seen to have played a determining role. However, on reflection one is likely to discover that even in such major decisions of one's life, a significant part has been played by unforeseen happenings, variously attributed to chance, coincidence, the influence of stars, Karma or Providence. One may even perceive that it was some apparently insignificant and chance events – such as meeting somebody, receiving a suggestion from someone or somewhere, coming across a book, visiting a certain place, etc. – that played a crucial role in shaping the course of one's life, though one hardly suspected the import of such seemingly inconsequential events at the time of their happening.[1] One is apt to realise that life is highly unpredictable and largely mysterious in its course.

A good deal of mystery and unpredictability often surrounds not only the events of our external lives, but

---

1. "A casual passing phrase can change our life." (Sri Aurobindo, *Savitri*, Sri Aurobindo Birth Centenary Library, Vol. 29, Pondicherry: Sri Aurobindo Ashram, 1970, p. 373.)

also what happens to us internally from day to day, sometimes even from hour to hour – the alternation of our moods, the upsurge of impulses, the kindling of emotions, changes in the state of our physical or psychological well-being, fluctuations in the level of our energy, etc. While some of these subjective changes may to some extent be explicable in terms of known external or internal factors, much of what happens within us is enigmatic.

According to those who can see behind the external appearances of things – mystics, yogis, occultists and the like – the key to such mystery behind the internal as well as external events and vicissitudes of our lives consists in the fact that all life is a play of hidden forces; we live and move in a world of forces of which we are almost totally unaware.

In a sense, all forces are secret, because, as Sri Aurobindo points out, all forces, whether physical or non-physical, are invisible. However, physical forces, such as electricity and magnetism, though invisible, are no longer a total secret to the civilized man as they were to the primitive, for science has discovered something of their nature through their outward manifestations and has therefore been able to harness them. Some of the psychological forces too, such as those attributed to the "unconscious", which were a secret to modern man before the discoveries of Freud and Jung, are now known to us to some extent, enabling us to formulate plausible though tentative hypotheses for the explanation of erstwhile mysterious phenomena such as those of hypnotism, hysteria, clairvoyance, etc. But from the viewpoint of what has been stated in this book regarding the host of forces that operate in the world, we still know little about the secret dynamics of life.

Our difficulty in discovering the forces of life is due to the nature of the normal or ordinary consciousness of the human being at the present point of his evolution. For the ordinary consciousness, which is mental, can apprehend things only through the sensorium, that is, the sensory and intellectual apparatus. Consequently, our knowledge of forces is indirect and limited to what the senses can perceive of the outward effects of forces and the intellectual inferences that can be drawn from such sensory perceptions. As Sri Aurobindo explains:

> "The ordinary consciousness is that in which one knows things only or mainly by the intellect, the external mind and the senses and knows forces etc. only by their outward manifestations and results and the rest by inferences from these data. There may be some play of mental intuition, deeper psychic seeing or impulsions, spiritual intimations, etc. – but in the ordinary consciousness these are incidental only and do not modify its fundamental character."[2]

It is when the consciousness develops and becomes more subtle that it comes into a more direct contact with the inner reality of things and gains an awareness of forces. In Sri Aurobindo's words:

> "The ordinary man lives in his own personal consciousness knowing things through his mind and senses as they are touched by a world which is outside him,

2. *Letters on Yoga*, Sri Aurobindo Birth Centenary Library, Vol. 22, (Pondicherry: Sri Aurobindo Ashram, 1970), p. 317.

outside his consciousness. When the consciousness subtilises, it begins to come into contact with things in a much more direct way, not only with their forms and outer impacts but with what is inside them, but still the range may be small. But the consciousness can also widen and begin to be first in direct contact with a universe of range of things in the world, then to contain them as it were, – as it is said to see the world in oneself, – and to be in a way identified with it. To see all things in the self and the self in all things – to be aware of one being everywhere, aware directly of the different planes, their forces, their beings – that is universalisation."[3]

"It [consciousness] begins to know inwardly and directly and not merely by external observation and contact the forces at play in the world, feels their movement, distinguishes their functioning and can operate immediately upon them as the scientist operates upon physical forces...."[4]

Such an inward and direct knowledge of things is the basis of what has been stated in the pages of this compilation regarding the hidden forces of life. Dealt with herein are the diverse forces which act on us, determining the course of events, influencing our thoughts, feelings and actions, affecting our moods, health and level of energy, pulling the human being to nether depths or beckoning him towards lofty heights. Spoken of in this

3. *Ibid.*
4. *The Synthesis of Yoga*, Sri Aurobindo Birth Centenary Library, Vol. 20, (Pondicherry: Sri Aurobindo Ashram, 1970), p. 172.

book are also the hidden forces behind evolution and beneficent forces which man can learn more and more to draw upon. Many of the passages in the book not only explain the nature of the various forces but also provide practical guidance in relation to both helpful as well as deleterious forces.

The powerful sway of life's hidden forces as described in this book shows that man's sense of possessing a free and independent will is highly illusory as long as one lives in the ordinary consciousness and is bound by the forces which impinge upon it. As Sri Aurobindo remarks:

> "The apparent freedom and self-assertion of our personal being to which we are so profoundly attached, conceal a most pitiable subjection to a thousand suggestions, impulses, forces which we have made extraneous to our little person. Our ego, boasting of freedom, is at every moment the slave, toy and puppet of countless beings, powers, forces, influences in universal Nature."[5]

However, what emerges from the contents of this compilation is not a gospel of fatalism, for, in the light of the secret dynamics of existence revealed herein, the forces of life in their overall action tend to subserve man's gradual growth out of the ordinary consciousness into progressively higher and deeper levels of being through the evolutionary process. For evolution, says Sri Aurobindo, consists in the ascent of the Spirit which, at first involved in Matter and inconscience, progressively

5. *Ibid.*, p. 53.

liberates itself by means of its secret evolutionary force, manifesting increasingly higher levels of its Consciousness. Having so far liberated Life and Mind out of Matter, the evolutionary impulse, says Sri Aurobindo, is already secretly at work here for ushering in the manifestation of what he terms the Supermind – the Truth-Consciousness beyond the level of Mind – thus preparing the dawn of a new world and the appearance of a new race of supramental beings. Therefore, though man in his ordinary state is depicted here as a creature who is more or less entirely moved and moulded by forces beyond his ken and control, Sri Aurobindo and the Mother have also given herein intimations of a marvellous future human destiny as not only a possibility but a promise.

A.S. DALAL

I

LIFE THROUGH THE EYE OF THE YOGIN

Nothing we think or do is void or vain;
Each is an energy loosed and holds its course.
The shadowy keepers of our deathless past
Have made our fate the child of our own acts,
And from the furrows laboured by our will
We reap the fruit of our forgotten deeds.
But since unseen the tree that bore this fruit
And we live in a present born from an unknown past,
They seem but parts of a mechanic Force,
To a mechanic mind tied by earth's laws;
Yet are they instruments of a Will supreme,
Watched by a still all-seeing Eye above.
A prescient architect of Fate and Chance
Who builds our lives on a foreseen design
The meaning knows and consequence of each step
And watches the inferior stumbling powers.

SRI AUROBINDO
Savitri, Book Four, Canto Three

For though a dress of blind and devious chance
Is laid upon the work of all-wise Fate,
Our acts interpret an omniscient Force
That dwells in the compelling stuff of things,
And nothing happens in the cosmic play
But at its time and in its foreseen place.

SRI AUROBINDO
Savitri, Book Five, Canto One

LIFE THROUGH THE EYE OF THE YOGIN

Play of Forces

Anyone with some intelligence and power of observation who lives more in an inward consciousness can see the play of invisible forces at every step which act on men and bring about events without their knowing about the instrumentation. The difference created by yoga or by an inner consciousness – for there are people like Socrates who develop or have some inner consciousness without yoga – is that one becomes conscious of these invisible forces and can also consciously profit by them or use and direct them. That is all.

SRI AUROBINDO

... the play of the forces is very complex and one has to be conscious of them and, as it were, see and watch how they work before one can really understand why things happen as they do.

SRI AUROBINDO

If we observe a happening, we judge and explain it from the result and from a glimpse of its most external constituents, circumstances or causes; but each happening is the outcome of a complex nexus of forces which we do not and cannot observe, because all forces are to us invisible, – but they are not invisible to the spiritual vision of the Infinite: some of them are actualities working to produce or occasion a new actuality, some are possibles that are near to the pre-existent actuals and in a way included in their aggregate; but there can intervene always new possibilities that suddenly become dynamic potentials and add themselves to the nexus, and behind all are imperatives or an imperative which these possibilities are labouring to actualise. Moreover, out of the same nexus of forces different results are possible; what will come out of them is determined by a sanction which was no doubt waiting and ready all the time but seems to come in rapidly to intervene and alter everything, a decisive divine imperative. All this our reason cannot grasp because it is the instrument of an ignorance with a very limited vision and a small stock of accumulated and not always very certain or reliable knowledge and because too it has no means of direct awareness; for this is the difference between intuition and intellect, that intuition is born of a direct awareness while intellect is an indirect action of a knowledge which constructs itself with difficulty out of the unknown from signs and indications and gathered data.

Sri Aurobindo

... there, [in the ordinary mind] there are only two categories of influences recognisable, the ideas and feelings and actions of oneself and others and the play of environment and physical forces. But once one begins to get the inner view of things, it is different. One begins to experience that all is an action of forces, forces of Prakriti psychological as well as physical, which play upon our nature – and these are conscious forces or are supported by a consciousness or consciousnesses behind. One is in the midst of a big universal working and it is impossible any longer to explain everything as the result of one's own sole and independent personality. You yourself have at one time written that your crises of despair etc. came upon you as if thrown on you and worked themselves out without your being able to determine or put an end to them. That means an action of universal forces and not merely an independent action of your own personality, though it is something in your nature of which they make use. But you are not conscious, and others also, of this intervention and pressure at its source for the reason I state.

SRI AUROBINDO

His new consciousness makes him feel more strongly the opposite forces that one contacts when one moves in the world and has to do affairs and meet with others and he is afraid of a response in the vital which will upset his sadhana or create difficulties. Evidently he is a man who is psychically sensitive or has become so to that thing which you blindly refuse to recognise even when you are in the midst of it – the play of forces. You can feel your friend's atmosphere through the letter "so beautiful, so strengthening, so refreshing" and it has an immediate effect on you. But your mind stares like an owl and wonders "What the hell can this be?", I suppose, because your medical books never told you about it and how can things be true which are not known either to the ordinary mind or science? It is by an incursion of an opposite kind of forces that you fall into the Old Man's clutches, but you can only groan and cry, "What's this?" and when they are swept aside in a moment by other forces blink and mutter,

"Well, that's funny!" Your friend can feel and know at once when he is being threatened by the opposite forces and so he can be on his guard and resist old Nick, because he can detect at once one of his principal means of attack.

SRI AUROBINDO

... looking at what happened in 1914 – or for that matter at all that is and has been happening in human history – the eye of the Yogin sees not only the outward events and persons and causes, but the enormous forces which precipitate them into action. If the men who fought were instruments in the hands of rulers and financiers, these in turn were mere puppets in the clutch of those forces. When one is habituated to see the things behind, one is no longer prone to be touched by the outward aspects – or to expect any remedy from political, institutional or social changes; the only way out is through the descent of a consciousness which is not the puppet of these forces but is greater than they are and can compel them either to change or disappear.

SRI AUROBINDO

... the First World War was the result of a tremendous descent of the forces of the vital world (hostile forces of the vital world) into the material world. Even those who were conscious of this descent and consequently armed to defend themselves against it, suffered from its consequences. The world, the whole earth suffered from its consequences. There was a general deterioration from the vital point of view, I could say, which was inevitable even for those who consciously knew whence the force came, whence the deterioration came, and who could therefore fight against it consciously – they could not prevent certain effects being produced in the earth atmosphere. Naturally, men do not know what happened to them; all that they have said is that everything had become worse since the war. That was all that they could affirm. For example, the moral level went down very much. It was simply the result of a formidable descent of the vital world: forces of disorder, forces of corruption, forces of deterioration, forces of destruction, forces of violence, forces of cruelty.

Why this descent?

Perhaps it was a reaction, for there was another Force coming down which wanted to do its work, and perhaps those forces did not want it – it disturbed their habits. It is like a government which fears that it will be thrown out and so intervenes violently in order to keep in power.

THE MOTHER

I have not said that everything is rigidly predetermined. Play of forces does not mean that. What I said was that behind visible events in the world there is always a mass of invisible forces at work unknown to the outward minds of men, and by yoga, (by going inward and establishing a conscious connection with the Cosmic Self and Force and forces,) one can become conscious of these forces, intervene consciously in the play, and to some extent at least determine things in the result of the play. All that has nothing to do with predetermination. On the contrary, one watches how things develop and gives a push here and a push there when possible or when needed. There is nothing in all that to contradict the dictum of the great scientist Sir C. V. Raman. Raman said once that all these scientific discoveries are only games of chance. Only, when he says that scientific discoveries are games of chance, he is merely saying that human beings don't know how it works out. It is not rigid predetermination, but it is not a blind inconscient Chance either. It is a play in which there is a working out of the possibilities in Time.

SRI AUROBINDO

All life is the play of universal forces. The individual gives a personal form to these universal forces. But he can choose whether he shall respond or not to the action of a particular force. Only most people do not really choose – they indulge the play of the forces. Your illnesses, depressions etc. are the repeated play of such forces. It is only when one can make oneself free of them that one can be the true person and have a true life – but one can be free only by living in the Divine.

SRI AUROBINDO

In the universal play there are some, the majority, who are ignorant instruments; they are actors who are moved about like puppets, knowing nothing. There are others who are conscious, and these act their part, knowing that it is a play. And there are some who have the full knowledge of the universal movement and are identified with it and with the one Divine Consciousness and yet consent to act as though they were something separate, a division of the whole. There are many intermediary stages between that ignorance and this full knowledge, many ways of participating in the play. There is a state of ignorance in which you do a thing and believe that it was you who decided it; there is a state of lesser ignorance in which you do it knowing that you are made to do it but you do not know how or why; and there is too a state of consciousness in which you are fully aware, – for you know what it is that acts through you, you know that you are an instrument, you know how and why your act is done, its process and its purpose. The state of ignorance in which you believe that you are the doer of your acts persists so long as it is necessary for your development; but as soon as you are capable of passing into a higher condition, you begin to see that you are an instrument of the one consciousness; you take a step upward and you rise to a higher conscious level.

THE MOTHER

Forces of Action and Reaction and Destiny

All energies put into activity – thought, speech, feeling, act – go to constitute Karma. These things help to develop the nature in one direction or another, and the nature and its actions and reactions produce their consequences inward and outward: they also act on others and create movements in the general sum of forces which can return upon oneself sooner or later. Thoughts unexpressed can also go out as forces and produce their effects. It is a mistake to think that a thought or will can have effect only when it is expressed in speech or act: the unspoken thought, the unexpressed will are also active energies and can produce their own vibrations, effects or reactions.

SRI AUROBINDO

Fundamentally, the meaning of Karma is that all existence is the working of a universal Energy, a process and an action and a building of things by that action, – an unbuilding too, but as a step to farther building, – that all is a continuous chain in which every one link is bound indissolubly to the past infinity of numberless links, and the whole governed by fixed relations, by a fixed association of cause and effect, present action the result of past action as future action will be the result of present action, all cause a working of energy and all effect too a working of energy. The moral significance is that all our existence is a putting out of an energy which is in us and by which we are made and as is the nature of the energy which is put forth as cause, so shall be that of the energy which returns as effect, that this is the universal law and nothing in the world can, being of and in our world, escape from its governing incidence.

SRI AUROBINDO

... if Karma be a universal truth or the universal truth of being, it must be equally true of the inly-born mental and moral worlds of our action as in our outward relations with the physical universe. It is the mental energy that we put forth which determines the mental effect, – but subject to all the impact of past, present and future surrounding circumstance, because we are not isolated powers in the world, but rather our energy a subordinate strain and thread of the universal energy. The moral energy of our action determines similarly the nature and effect of the moral consequence, but subject too, – though to this element the rigid moralist does not give sufficient consideration, – to the same incidence of past, present and future surrounding circumstance. That this is true of the output of physical energy, needs no saying nor any demonstration. We must recognise these different types and variously formulated motions of the one universal Force, and it will not do to say from the beginning that the measure and quality of my inner being is some result of the output of a physical energy translated into mental and moral energies, – for instance, that my doing a good or a bad action or yielding to good or to bad affections and motives is at the mercy of my liver, or contained in the physical germ of my birth, or is the effect of my chemical elements or determined essentially and ultimately by the disposition of the constituent electrons of my brain and nervous system. Whatever drafts my mental and moral being may make on the corporeal for its supporting physical energy and however it may be affected by its borrowings, yet it is very evident that it uses them for other and larger purposes, has a supraphysical method, evolves much greater motives and significances. The moral energy is in itself a distinct power, has its own plane of Karma, moves me even, and that characteristically, to override my vital and physical nature. Forms of one universal Force at bottom – or at top – these may be, but in practice they are different energies and have to be so dealt with – until we can find what that universal Force may be in its highest purest texture and initial power and whether that discovery can give us in the perplexities of our nature a unifying direction.

SRI AUROBINDO

The laws of being are at bottom one for all of us, because all existence is one existence; one Spirit, one self, one mind, one life, one energy of process is at work; one will and wisdom has planned or has evolved from itself the whole business of creation. And yet in this oneness there is a persistent variety, which we see first in the form of a communal variation. There is everywhere a group-energy, group-life, group-mind, and if soul is, then we have reason to believe that however elusive it may be to our seizing, there is a group-soul which is the support and foundation – some would call it the result – of this communal variety. That gives us a ground for a group-karma. For the group or collective soul renews and prolongs itself and in man at least develops its nature and experience from generation to generation. And who knows whether, when one form of it is disintegrated, community or nation, it may not wait for and assume other forms in which its will of being, its type of nature and mentality, its attempt of experience is carried forward, migrates, one might almost say, into new-born collective bodies, in other ages or cycles? Mankind itself has this separate collective soul and collective existence. And on that community the community of Karma is founded; the action and development of the whole produces consequence of Karma and experience for the individual and the totality even as the action and development of the individual produces consequences and experience for others, for the group, for the whole.

SRI AUROBINDO

Many astrological predictions come true, quite a mass of them, if one takes all together. But it does not follow that the stars rule our destiny; the stars merely record a destiny that has been already formed, they are a hieroglyph, not a Force, – or if their action constitutes a force, it is a transmitting energy, not an originating Power. Someone is there who has determined or something is there which is Fate, let us say; the stars are only indicators. The astrologers themselves say that there are two forces, *daiva* and *puruṣakāra*, fate and individual energy, and the individual energy can modify and even frustrate fate. Moreover, the stars often indicate several fate-possibilities; for example that one may die in mid-age, but that if that determination can be overcome, one can live to a predictable old age. Finally, cases are seen in which the predictions of the horoscope fulfil themselves with great accuracy up to a certain age, then apply no more. This often happens when the subject turns away from the ordinary to the spiritual life. If the turn is very radical, the cessation of predictability may be immediate; otherwise certain results may still last on for a time, but there is no longer the same inevitability. This would seem to show that there is or can be a higher power or higher plane or higher source of spiritual destiny which can, if its hour has come, override the lower power, lower plane or lower source of vital and material fate of which the stars are indicators. I say vital because character can also be indicated from the horoscope much more completely and satisfactorily than the events of the life.

The Indian explanation of fate is Karma. We ourselves are our own fate through our actions, but the fate created by us binds us; for what we have sown, we must reap in this life or another. Still we are creating our fate for the future even while undergoing old fate from the past in the present. That gives a meaning to our will and action and does not, as European critics wrongly believe, constitute a rigid and sterilising fatalism. But again, our will and action can often annul or modify even the past Karma, it is only certain strong effects, called *utkaṭa karma*, that are non-modifiable. Here too the achievement of the spiritual consciousness and life is supposed to annul or give the power to annul Karma. For we enter into union with the Will Divine, cosmic or transcendent, which can annul what it had sanctioned for certain conditions, new-create what it had created, the narrow fixed lines disappear, there is a more plastic freedom and wideness. Neither Karma nor Astrology therefore points to a rigid and for ever immutable fate.

Sri Aurobindo

I must, however, guard against the idea that the signs and planets determine a man's character or fate. They do not, they only indicate it, because they are the sensational, celestial and astral influences or nervous force in Nature which become the instruments of our Karma. That is why the European mystics gave the name of astral planes to the plane of sensational or nervous existence and astral fluid to the magnetic power or current of nervous vital force in a man. It is this same vital force which pours upon us from all parts of the solar system and of this physical universe. But man is mightier than his sensations or vitality or the sensational or vital forces of the universe. Our fate and our temperament have been built by our own wills and our own wills can alter them.

Sri Aurobindo

In Indian astrology which considers all life-circumstances to be Karma, mostly predetermined or indicated in the graph of the stars, there is still provision made for the energy and force of the being which can change or cancel part or much of what is so written or even all but the most imperative and powerful bindings of Karma. This is a reasonable account of the balance: but there is also to be added to the computation the fact that destiny is not simple but complex; the destiny which binds our physical being, binds it so long or in so far as a greater law does not intervene. Action belongs to the physical part of us, it is the physical outcome of our being; but behind our surface is a freer Life-power, a freer Mind-power which has another energy and can create another destiny and bring it in to modify the primary plan, and when the soul and self emerges, when we become consciously spiritual beings, that change can cancel or wholly remodel the graph of our physical fate. Karma, then, – or at least any mechanical law of Karma, – cannot be accepted as the sole determinant of circumstances and the whole machinery of rebirth and of our future evolution.

Sri Aurobindo

Forces in Human Interchange

There is a constant mental, vital, subtle-physical interchange going on between all who meet or live together, of which they are themselves unaware except in so far as its impacts and interpenetrations touch them as sensible results of speech and action and outer contact: for the most part it is subtly and invisibly that this interchange takes place; for it acts indirectly, touching the subliminal parts and through them the outer nature. But when we grow conscious in these subliminal parts, that brings consciousness also of all this interaction and subjective interchange and intermingling, with the result that we need no longer be involuntary subjects of their impact and consequence, but can accept or reject, defend ourselves or isolate. At the same time, our action on others need no longer be ignorant or involuntary and often unintentionally harmful; it can be a conscious help, a luminous interchange and a fruitful accommodation, an approach towards an inner understanding or union, not as now a separative association with only a limited intimacy or unity, restricted by much non-understanding and often burdened or endangered by a mass of misunderstanding, of mutual misinterpretation and error.

Sri Aurobindo

There is always a drawing of vital forces from one to another in all human social mixture that takes place automatically. Love-making is one of the most powerful ways of each drawing upon the other's vital force, or of one drawing the other's, which also often happens in a one-sided way to the great detriment of the "other". In the passage come many things good and bad, elation, feeling of strength and support, infiltration of good or bad qualities, interchange of psychological moods, states and movements, depressions, exhaustion – the whole gamut. People don't know it – which is a mercy of God upon them – but when one gets into a certain yogic consciousness, one becomes very much aware and sensitive to all this interchange and action and reaction, but also one can build a wall against, reject etc. etc.

It is a wall of consciousness that one has to build. Consciousness is not something abstract, it is like existence itself or Ananda or mind or *prāṇa*, something very concrete. If one becomes aware of the inner consciousness, one can do all sorts of things with it, send it out as a stream of force, erect a circle or wall of consciousness around oneself, direct an idea so that it shall enter somebody's head in America etc. etc.

SRI AUROBINDO

No, people are not conscious of these things, only a few are. The vital exchange is there, but they are not aware of it – because they live in the external mind (physical) and these things go on behind. Even if they feel more energetic after an interchange or depressed or tired, they would not attribute it to the talk or contact, because the interchange is unconscious; their external mind in which they live not being aware of it.

SRI AUROBINDO

I don't suppose people are at all aware of this occult commerce. Some like Daudet may observe the expenditure or throwing out of forces, but not the pulling or the effect on others. The idea of mental interchange is familiar though only of the superficial kind, not the silent action of mind on mind which is always going on, but the vital impacts are known only to a few occultists. If one becomes very conscious one can become aware of the forces acting in and from all around, e.g. forces of joy or depression or anger.

SRI AUROBINDO

It is not necessary to be so careful as all that. Ordinary vital interchanges are of a slight character. Nobody can take away another's vital, for the very good reason that if that happened, the person from whom it was taken would die. It is possible of course for one person to drain another's vital forces so as to leave him limp or weak or dry, but it is only the vampire kind that do that. It is possible also for one to give out too much of one's vital forces so as to weaken oneself or exhaust of energy, a thing which should not be done, – it is only those who know how to draw or can draw freely from the universal vital Force and replenish their life energies that can give out freely. All of course draw to some extent, otherwise they would not remain alive, for expenditure of vital energy is always going on and one has to replace it; but for most the capacity for drawing is limited and the capacity for giving without exhaustion is also limited.

But the ordinary movements of interchange are harmless provided they are kept within moderate limits.

SRI AUROBINDO

When people mix together there is generally some inter-change of vital forces which is quite involuntary.... Vampirising is a special phenomenon – a person who lives upon the vital of others and flourishes vitally at their expense.

SRI AUROBINDO

The tired feeling which the people felt after seeing this X is a sign of vampirism, but very often there is no such feeling but there is an after-effect on the whole. The nerves get gradually wrong – what is called the nervous envelope becomes weak or in one way or another the vitality becomes weak or gets into an abnormal condition – excitable and irritable. There are many such ways in which the effect shows itself. Sex-vampirism is a different matter – in sex interchange the normal thing is to give and take, but the sex-vampire eats up the other's vital and gives nothing or very little.

SRI AUROBINDO

Every letter means an interchange with the person who writes it – for something is there behind the words, something of his person or of the forces he has put out or had around him while writing. Our thoughts and feelings are also forces and can have effects upon others. One has to grow conscious of the movement of these forces and then one can control one's own mental and vital forma-tions and cease to be affected by those of others.

SRI AUROBINDO

Human Will, Nature-Force and Divine Will

… at least nine-tenths of our freedom of will is a palpable fiction; that will is created and determined not by its own self-existent action at a given moment, but by our past, our heredity, our training, our environment, the whole tremendous complex thing we call Karma, which is, behind us, the whole past action of Nature on us and the world converging in the individual, determining what he is, determining what his will shall be at a given moment and determining, as far as analysis can see, even its action at that moment. The ego associates itself always with its Karma and it says "I did" and "I will" and "I suffer", but if it looks at itself and sees how it was made, it is obliged to say of man as of the animal, "Nature did this in me, Nature wills in me", and if it qualifies by saying "my Nature", that only means "Nature as self-determined in this individual creature". It was the strong perception of this aspect of existence which compelled the Buddhists to declare that all is Karma and that there is no self in existence, that the idea of self is only a delusion of the ego-mind.

SRI AUROBINDO

In reality, the freedom and the determination are only two sides of the same thing – for the fundamental truth is self-determination of the cosmos and in it a secret self-determination of the individual. The difficulty arises from the fact that we live in the surface mind of ignorance, do not know what is going on behind and see only the phenomenal process of Nature. There the apparent fact is an overwhelming determinism of Nature and as our surface consciousness is part of that process, we are unable to see the other term of the biune reality. For practical purposes, on the surface there is an entire determinism in Matter – though this is now disputed by the latest school of Science. As Life emerges a certain plasticity sets in, so that it is difficult to predict anything exactly as one predicts material things that obey a rigid law. The plasticity increases with the growth of Mind, so that man can have at least a sense of free-will, of a choice of his action, of a self-movement which at least helps to determine circumstances. But this freedom is dubious because it can be declared to be an illusion, a device of Nature, part of its machinery of determination, only a seeming freedom or at most a restricted, relative and subject independence. It is only when one goes behind away from Prakriti to Purusha and upward away from Mind to spiritual Self that the side of freedom comes to be first evident and then, by unison with the Will which is above Nature, complete.

SRI AUROBINDO

The only free will in the world is the one divine Will of which Nature is the executrix; for she is the master and creator of all other wills. Human free will can be real in a sense, but, like all things that belong to the modes of Nature, it is only relatively real. The mind rides on a swirl of natural forces, balances on a poise between several possibilities, inclines to one side or another, settles and has the sense of choosing: but it does not see, it is not even dimly aware of the Force behind that has determined its choice. It cannot see it, because that Force is something total and to our eyes indeterminate. At most mind can only distinguish with an approach to clarity and precision some out of the complex variety of particular determinations by which this Force works out her incalculable purposes. Partial itself, the mind rides on a part of the machine, unaware of nine-tenths of its motor agencies in Time and environment, unaware of its past preparation and future drift; but because it rides, it thinks that it is directing the machine. In a sense it counts: for that clear inclination of the mind which we call our will, that firm settling of the inclination which presents itself to us as a deliberate choice, is one of Nature's most powerful determinants; but it is never independent and sole. Behind this petty instrumental action of the human will there is something vast and powerful and eternal that oversees the trend of the inclination and presses on the turn of the will. There is a total Truth in Nature greater than our individual choice. And in this total Truth, or even beyond and behind it, there is something that determines all results; its presence and secret knowledge keep up steadily in the process of Nature, a dynamic, almost automatic perception of the right relations, the varying or persistent necessities, the inevitable steps of the movement. There is a secret divine Will, eternal and infinite, omniscient and omnipotent, that expresses itself in the universality and in each particular of all these apparently temporal and finite, inconscient or half-conscient things. This is the Power or Presence meant by the Gita when it speaks of the Lord within the heart of all existences who turns all creatures as if mounted on a machine by the illusion of Nature.

SRI AUROBINDO

This apparently self-acting mechanism of Nature conceals an immanent divine Will that compels and guides it and shapes its purposes. But you cannot feel or know that Will while you are shut up in your narrow cell of personality, blinded and chained to your viewpoint of the ego and its desires. For you can wholly respond to it only when you are impersonalised by knowledge and widened to see all things in the self and in God and the self and God in all things. All becomes here by the power of the Spirit; all do their works by the immanence of God in things and his presence in the heart of every creature.

SRI AUROBINDO

... what is this divine supreme Will and how can it be recognised by our deluded instruments and our blind prisoned intelligence?

Ordinarily, we conceive of ourselves as a separate "I" in the universe that governs a separate body and mental and moral nature, chooses in full liberty its own self-determined actions and is independent and therefore sole master of its works and responsible. It is not easy for the ordinary mind, the mind that has not thought nor looked deeply into its own constitution and constituents, it is difficult even for minds that have thought but have no spiritual vision and experience, to imagine how there can be anything else in us truer, deeper and more powerful than this apparent "I" and its empire. But the very first step towards self-knowledge as towards the true knowledge of phenomena is to get behind the apparent truth of things and find the real but masked, essential and dynamic truth which their appearances cover.

This ego or "I" is not a lasting truth, much less our essential part; it is only a formation of Nature, a mental form of thought-centralisation in the perceiving and discriminating mind, a vital form of the centralisation of feeling and sensation in our parts of life, a form of physical conscious reception centralising substance and function of substance in our bodies. All that we internally are is not ego, but consciousness, soul or spirit. All that we externally and superficially are and do is not ego but Nature. An executive cosmic force shapes us and dictates through our temperament and environment and mentality so shaped, through our individualised formulation of the cosmic energies, our actions and their results. Truly, we do not think, will or act but thought occurs in us, will occurs in us, impulse and act occur in us; our ego-sense gathers around itself, refers to itself all this flow of natural activities. It is cosmic Force, it is Nature that forms the thought, imposes the will, imparts the impulse. Our body, mind and ego are a wave of that sea of force in action and do not govern it, but by it are governed and directed. The Sadhaka in his progress towards truth and self-knowledge must come to a point where the soul opens its eyes of vision and recognises this truth of ego and this truth of works. He gives up the idea of a mental, vital, physical "I" that acts or governs action; he recognises that Prakriti, Force of cosmic nature following her fixed modes, is in him and in all things and creatures the one and only worker.

SRI AUROBINDO

The universal forces move by their own force and the consciousness within them – but there is also the Cosmic

Spirit who supports them and determines by his onlook and disposing will their play – although the direct action is left to the forces – it is the play of universal Prakriti with the universal Purusha watching behind it. In the individual also there is the individual Purusha who can, if he wills, not merely assent to the play of Prakriti, but accept or reject or will for its change. All that is in the play itself as we see it here. There is something above – but the action of that is an intervention rather than a moment to moment control; it can become a constant direct control only when one replaces the play of the forces by the government of the Divine.

SRI AUROBINDO

The Cosmic Divine is what is concerned with the actual working out of things under the present circumstances. It is the Will of that Cosmic Divine which is manifested in each circumstance, each movement of this world.

The Cosmic Will is not, to our ordinary consciousness, something that acts as an independent power doing whatever it chooses; it works through all these beings, through the forces at play in the world and the law of these forces and their results – it is only when we open ourselves and get out of the ordinary consciousness that we can feel it intervening as an independent power and overriding the ordinary play of the forces.

Then too we can see that even in the play of the forces and in spite of their distortions the Cosmic Will is working towards the eventual realisation of the Will of the Transcendent Divine.

SRI AUROBINDO

II

HIDDEN FORCES WITHIN

Only a little of us foresees its steps,
Only a little has will and purposed pace.
A vast subliminal is man's measureless part.
The dim subconscient is his cavern base.

SRI AUROBINDO
Savitri, Book Seven, Canto Two

A portion of us lives in present Time,
A secret mass in dim inconscience gropes;
Out of the inconscient and subliminal
Arisen, we live in mind's uncertain light
And strive to know and master a dubious world
Whose purpose and meaning are hidden from our sight.
Above us dwells a superconscient god
Hidden in the mystery of his own light:
Around us is a vast of ignorance
Lit by the uncertain ray of human mind,
Below us sleeps the Inconscient dark and mute.

Ibid.

HIDDEN FORCES WITHIN

The Subconscient, the Subliminal and the Superconscient

It is a mistake to think that we live physically only, with the outer mind and life. We are all the time living and acting on other planes of consciousness, meeting others there and acting upon them, and what we do and feel and think there, the forces we gather, the results we prepare have an incalculable importance and effect, unknown to us, upon our outer life. Not all of it comes through, and what comes through takes another form in the physical – though sometimes there is an exact correspondence; but this little is at the basis of our outward existence. All that we become and do and bear in the physical life is prepared behind the veil within us. It is therefore of immense importance for a yoga which aims at the transformation of life to grow conscious of what goes on within these domains, to be master there and be able to feel, know and deal with the secret forces that determine our destiny and our internal and external growth or decline.

SRI AUROBINDO

A superficial observation of our waking consciousness shows us that of a great part of our individual being and becoming we are quite ignorant; it is to us the Inconscient, just as much as the life of the plant, the metal, the earth, the elements. But if we carry our knowledge farther, pushing psychological experiment and observation beyond their normal bounds, we find how vast is the sphere of this supposed Inconscient or this subconscient in

our total existence, – the subconscient, so seeming and so
called by us because it is a concealed consciousness, – and
what a small and fragmentary portion of our being is
covered by our waking self-awareness. We arrive at the
knowledge that our waking mind and ego are only a
superimposition upon a submerged, a subliminal self, –
for so that self appears to us, – or, more accurately, an
inner being, with a much vaster capacity of experience;
our mind and ego are like the crown and dome of a temple
jutting out from the waves while the great body of the
building is submerged under the surface of the waters.

This concealed self and consciousness is our real or
whole being, of which the outer is a part and a phenomenon, a selective formation for a surface use. We
perceive only a small number of the contacts of things
which impinge upon us; the inner being perceives all that
enters or touches us and our environment. We perceive
only a part of the workings of our life and being; the inner
being perceives so much that we might almost suppose
that nothing escapes its view. We remember only a small
selection from our perceptions, and of these even we keep
a great part in a store-room where we cannot always lay
our hand upon what we need; the inner being retains
everything that it has ever received and has it always ready
to hand. We can form into co-ordinated understanding
and knowledge only so much of our perceptions and
memories as our trained intelligence and mental capacity
can grasp in their sense and appreciate in their relations:
the intelligence of the inner being needs no training, but
preserves the accurate form and relations of all its perceptions and memories and, – though this is a proposition
which may be considered doubtful or difficult to concede

in its fullness, – can grasp immediately, when it does not possess already, their significance. And its perceptions are not confined, as are ordinarily those of the waking mind, to the scanty gleanings of the physical senses, but extend far beyond and use, as telepathic phenomena of many kinds bear witness, a subtle sense the limits of which are too wide to be easily fixed. The relations between the surface will or impulsion and the subliminal urge, mistakenly described as unconscious or subconscious, have not been properly studied except in regard to unusual and unorganised manifestations and to certain morbidly abnormal phenomena of the diseased human mind; but if we pursue our observation far enough, we shall find that the cognition and will or impulsive force of the inner being really stand behind the whole conscious becoming; the latter represents only that part of its secret endeavour and achievement which rises successfully to the surface of our life. To know our inner being is the first step towards a real self-knowledge.

If we undertake this self-discovery and enlarge our knowledge of the subliminal self, so conceiving it as to include in it our lower subconscient and upper superconscient ends, we shall discover that it is really this which provides the whole material of our apparent being and that our perceptions, our memories, our effectuations of will and intelligence are only a selection from its perceptions, memories, activities and relations of will and intelligence; our very ego is only a minor and superficial formulation of its self-consciousness and self-experience. It is, as it were, the urgent sea out of which the waves of our conscious becoming arise.

SRI AUROBINDO

There are three occult sources of our action – the super-conscient, the subliminal, the subconscient, but of none of them are we in control or even aware. What we are aware of is the surface being which is only an instrumental arrangement. The source of all is the general Nature, – universal Nature individualising itself in each person; for this general Nature deposits certain habits of movement, personality, character, faculties, dispositions, tendencies in us, and that, whether formed now or before our birth, is what we usually call ourselves. A good deal of this is in habitual movement and use in our known conscious parts on the surface, a great deal more is concealed in the other unknown three which are below or behind the surface.

But what we are on the surface is being constantly set in motion, changed, developed or repeated by the waves of the general Nature coming in on us either directly or else indirectly through others, through circumstances, through various agencies or channels. Some of this flows straight into the conscious parts and acts there, but our mind ignores its source, appropriates it and regards all that as its own; a part comes secretly into the subconscient or sinks into it and waits for an opportunity of rising up into the conscious surface; a good deal goes into the subliminal and may at any time come out – or may not, may rather rest there as unused matter. Part passes through and is rejected, thrown back or thrown out or spilt into the universal sea. Our nature is a constant activity of forces supplied to us out of which (or rather out of a small amount of it) we make what we will or can. What we make seems fixed and formed for good, but in reality it is all a play of forces, a flux, nothing fixed or stable; the appearance of stability is given by constant repetition and recurrence of the same vibrations and formations.

SRI AUROBINDO

We are not only what we know of ourselves but an immense more which we do not know; our momentary personality is only a bubble on the ocean of our existence.

SRI AUROBINDO

... what we know of ourselves, our present conscious existence, is only a representative formation, a superficial activity, a changing external result of a vast mass of concealed existence. Our visible life and the actions of that life are no more than a series of significant expres·sions, but that which it tries to express is not on the surface; our existence is something much larger than this apparent frontal being which we suppose ourselves to be and which we offer to the world around us. This frontal and external being is a confused amalgam of mind-formations, life-movements, physical functionings of which even an exhaustive analysis into its component parts and machinery fails to reveal the whole secret. It is only when we go behind, below, above into the hidden stretches of our being that we can know it; the most thorough and acute surface scrutiny and manipulation cannot give us the true understanding or the completely effective control of our life, its purposes, its activities; that inability indeed is the cause of the failure of reason, morality and every other surface action to control and deliver and perfect the life of the human race. For below even our most obscure physical consciousness is a subconscious being in which as in a covering and supporting soil are all manner of hidden seeds that sprout up, unaccountably to us, on our surface and into which we are constantly throwing fresh seeds that prolong our past and will influence our future, – a subconscious being, obscure, small in its motions, capriciously and almost fantastically subrational, but of immense potency for the earth-life. Again behind our mind, our life, our conscious physical there is a large subliminal consciousness, – there are inner mental, inner vital, inner more subtle physical reaches supported by an inmost psychic existence which is the connecting soul of all the rest; and in these hidden reaches too lie a mass of numerous pre-existent personalities which supply the material, the motive-forces, the impulsions of our developing surface existence. For in each one of us here there may be one central person, but also a multitude of subordinate personalities created by the past history of its manifestation or by expressions of it on these inner planes which support its present play in this external material cosmos. And while on our surface we are cut off from all around us except through an exterior mind and sense-contact which delivers but little of us to our world or of our world to us, in these inner reaches the barrier between us and the rest of existence is thin and easily broken; there we can feel at once – not merely infer from their results, but feel directly – the action of the secret world-forces, mind-forces, life-forces, subtle physical forces that constitute universal and individual existence; we shall even be able, if we will but train ourselves to it, to lay our hands on these world-forces that throw themselves on us or around us and more and more to control or at least strongly modify their action on us and others, their formations, their very movements. Yet again above our human mind are still greater reaches superconscient to it and from there secretly descend influences, powers, touches which are the original determinants of things here and, if they were called down in their fullness, could altogether alter the whole make and economy of life in the material universe.

SRI AUROBINDO

... we mean by the subconscient that quite submerged part of our being in which there is no wakingly conscious and coherent thought, will or feeling or organized reaction, but which yet receives obscurely the impressions of all things and stores them up in itself and from it too all sorts of stimuli, of persistent habitual movements, crudely repeated or disguised in strange forms can surge up into dream or into the waking nature. For if these impressions rise up most in dream in an incoherent and disorganized manner, they can also and do rise up into our waking consciousness as a mechanical repetition of old thoughts, old mental, vital and physical habits or an obscure stimulus to sensations, actions, emotions which do not originate in or from our conscious thought or will and are even often opposed to its perceptions, choice or dictates. In the subconscient there is an obscure mind full of obstinate Sanskaras, impressions, associations, fixed notions, habitual reactions formed by our past, an obscure vital full of the seeds of habitual desires, sensations and nervous reactions, a most obscure material which governs much that has to do with the condition of the body. It is largely responsible for our illnesses; chronic or repeated illnesses are indeed mainly due to the subconscient and its obstinate memory and habit of repetition of whatever has impressed itself upon the body-consciousness. But this subconscient must be clearly distinguished from the subliminal parts of our being such as the inner or subtle physical consciousness, the inner vital or inner mental; for these are not at all obscure or incoherent or ill-organized, but only veiled from our surface consciousness. Our surface constantly receives something, inner touches, communications or influences, from these sources but does not know for the most part whence they come.

SRI AUROBINDO

The subconscient is a concealed and unexpressed inarticulate consciousness which works below all our conscious physical activities. Just as what we call the superconscient is really a higher consciousness above from which things descend into the being, so the subconscient is below the body-consciousness and things come up into the physical, the vital and the mind-nature from there.

Just as the higher consciousness is superconscient to us and supports all our spiritual possibilities and nature, so the subconscient is the basis of our material being and supports all that comes up in the physical nature.

Men are not ordinarily conscious of either of these planes of their own being, but by sadhana they can become aware.

The subconscient retains the impressions of all our past experiences of life and they can come up from there in dream forms: most dreams in ordinary sleep are formations made from subconscient impressions.

The habit of strong recurrence of the same things in our physical consciousness, so that it is difficult to get rid of its habits, is largely due to a subconscient support. The subconscient is full of irrational habits.

When things are rejected from all other parts of the nature, they go either into the environmental consciousness around us through which we communicate with others and with universal Nature and try to return from there or they sink into the subconscient and can come up from there even after lying long quiescent so that we think they are gone.

When something is erased from the subconscient so completely that it leaves no seed and thrown out of the circumconscient so completely that it can return no more, then only can we be sure that we have finished with it for ever.

SRI AUROBINDO

Mother, there are people who suffer from certain illnesses year after year, we know. Now, if we observe this illness, we see that it comes at a particular time of the year and this goes on the next year also, and it is like that. But the time is fixed. Then what is the reason, and how can one get rid of this?

There could be many reasons. It depends on the person you ask. If you ask an astrologer he will tell you, "It is the stars, when the stars come into the same position, the same conditions recur." Well, this is not so wrong. It can be like that. It can also be the individual's reaction to certain types of climate, you see, or to the sun's position;

or it may be quite simply a bad habit. That's all.
(*Laughter*).

And if one forms... If by chance it has happened to you
twice consecutively, then you form... you have a good
formation, you see, which remains like that (*gesture*) in
the subconscient, without showing itself – if you don't
observe it! And then, just when the time draws near, quite
gently it pushes up from within and tells you, "Take care,
the time is coming, the time is coming, the time is
coming!" So naturally, that comes along too. Usually
these things are like that.

But almost everything that happens in the physical is
like that. The first time it may be quite simply a concur-
rence of circumstances; then, the mind intervenes and
makes a construction. Now, if one accepts the construction, one is sure that it functions with clockwork precision.
But even if one says, "Oh, nonsense, it is only an idea!"
and does this (*gesture*), still the idea, instead of going
away, enters inside, into the subconscient, simply the
subconscious mind, and there it remains quietly. And
then, when the time comes to manifest itself, from inside,
like this, it makes a kind of... as though it were tickling the
memory a little, nothing more than that, just that. If it
rubs the memory just a little, like that, then suddenly one
day you remember: "Why, last year, at this time I was ill."
And crash! There it is, it has entered. It has entered the
zone of the active consciousness, and a few days later the
thing happens.

But when you have had either an experience or, like
this, some kind of phenomenon or an illness (above all in
the case of illness or even an accident), the body remembers for a very long time. If you want to be completely

cured, you must cure this memory in the body, this is absolutely indispensable. And whether you know it or not, you work in order to cure the memory in the body. When the remembrance is effaced, the body is truly healed.

Unfortunately, instead of destroying the remembrance, you push it back. Most of the time you push it down into the subconscient and sometimes into the inconscient, still more deep. Well now, if it is pushed back, if it is not completely effaced, then very gently, very gently, without seeming to do so at all it comes up to the surface; and something of which you have been cured for years, if by chance it crosses your mind simply like that, just like a little dart, as fast as that, like a passing dart: "Why, at this time I had that", you may be sure that sooner or later – a few seconds, a few minutes, a few hours or days later, it will return. You can... It may come back in a much milder form, it may come back in the same form, it may come even more strongly. That depends on your inner state. If you are in a pessimistic state, it will come back more strongly. If you are in an optimistic state, it will be much weaker. But it will come back and you will have to begin the battle all over again against the memory of your body so as to destroy it –if this time you are more attentive. If you can destroy it, you are cured. But if you don't destroy it, it will return. It will take a longer or shorter time, it will be more or less total, but it will return. It can come back in a flash. If you are wide awake and, when it returns, if you have enough knowledge and indeed enough clear-sighted-ness to tell yourself, "Well, here is that wretched remem-brance come back again to play its tricks", then you can give, can strike a violent blow and indeed destroy its reality. If you know how to do this, then it is an opportunity to get rid of the thing immediately. But it is not very easy to do this.

Pavitra: *How to do it?*

How to do it? (*Mother laughs.*) How to do it? It is the same thing as, the same method as, knowing how to destroy a formation, you understand.

It is a certain strength to dissolve things, which can undo formations. It depends on the nature of the formation. If it is like this, a formation of an adverse kind, then you need the force of a perfectly pure constructive light. If you have this at your disposal, all that you have to do is to bombard the thing with it, and you can dissolve it. But it is an operation which must be performed with inner forces; it cannot be done physically.

That is why all physical remedies, you see, are simply palliatives; they are not cures, because they are not strong enough to touch the living centre of the thing.

(*Silence*)

The same phenomenon occurs with moral difficulties. If one could succeed in destroying their remembrance, destroying in oneself the memory of the state one is in when in that difficulty, if one is sincere it would be the end of all difficulties for ever.

THE MOTHER

One is born with a slough to clean before one begins to live. And once you have made a good start on the way to the inner transformation and you go down to the subconscient root of the being – that exactly which comes from parents, from atavism – well, you do see what it is! And all, almost all difficulties are there, there are very few things added to existence after the first years of life. This happens at any odd moment; if you keep bad company or read bad books, the poison may enter you; but there are all the imprints deep-rooted in the subconscient, the dirty habits you have and against which you struggle. For instance, there are people who can't open their mouth without telling a lie, and they don't always do this deliberately (that is the worst of it), or people who can't come in touch with others without quarrelling, all sorts of stupidities – they are there in the subconscient, deeply rooted. Now, when you have a goodwill, externally you do your best to avoid all that, to correct it if possible; you work, you fight; then become aware that this thing always keeps coming up, it comes up from some part which escapes your control. But if you enter this subconscient, if you let your consciousness infiltrate it, and look carefully, gradually you will discover all the sources, all the origins of all your difficulties; then you will begin to understand what your fathers and mothers, grandfathers and grandmothers were, and if at a certain moment you are unable to control yourself, you will understand, "I am like that because they were like that."

THE MOTHER

Our waking state is unaware of its connection with the subliminal being, although it receives from it, – but without any knowledge of the place of origin, – the inspirations, intuitions, ideas, will-suggestions, sense-suggestions, urges to action that rise from below or from behind our limited surface existence. Sleep like trance opens the gate of the subliminal to us; for in sleep, as in trance, we retire behind the veil of the limited waking personality and it is behind this veil that the subliminal has its existence. But we receive the records of our sleep experience through dream and in dream figures and not in that condition which might be called an inner waking and which is the most accessible form of the trance state, nor through the supernormal clarities of vision and other more luminous and concrete ways of communication developed by the inner subliminal cognition when it gets into habitual or occasional conscious connection with our waking self. The subliminal, with the subconscious as an annexe of itself, – for the subconscious is also part of the behind-the-veil entity, – is the seer of inner things and of supraphysical experiences; the surface subconscious is only a transcriber. It is for this reason that the Upanishad describes the subliminal being as the Dream Self because it is normally in dreams, visions, absorbed states of inner experience that we enter into and are part of its experiences, – just as it describes the superconscient as the Sleep Self because normally all mental or sensory experiences cease when we enter this superconscience. For in the deeper trance into which the touch of the superconscient plunges our mentality, no record from it or transcript of its contents can normally reach us; it is only by an especial or an unusual development, in a supernormal condition or through a break or rift in our confined normality, that we can be on the surface conscious of the contacts or messages of the Superconscience.

SRI AUROBINDO

... from there [the subliminal] come all the greater aspirations, ideals, strivings towards a better self and better humanity without which man would be only a thinking animal – as also most of the art, poetry, philosophy, thirst for knowledge which relieve, if they do not yet dispel, the ignorance.

The role of the superconscient has been to evolve slowly the spiritual man out of the mental half-animal.

SRI AUROBINDO

Even in Europe the existence of something behind the surface is now very frequently admitted, but its nature is mistaken and it is called subconscient or subliminal, while really it is very conscious in its own way and not subliminal but only behind the veil. It is, according to our psychology, connected with the small outer personality by certain centres of consciousness of which we become aware by yoga. Only a little of the inner being escapes through these centres into the outer life, but that little is the best part of ourselves and responsible for our art, poetry, philosophy, ideals, religious aspirations, efforts at knowledge and perfection.

SRI AUROBINDO

The Psychic

At the beginning the soul in Nature, the psychic entity, whose unfolding is the first step towards a spiritual change, is an entirely veiled part of us, although it is that by which we exist and persist as individual beings in Nature. The other parts of our natural composition are not only mutable but perishable; but the psychic entity in us persists and is fundamentally the same always: it contains all essential possibilities of our manifestation but is not constituted by them; it is not limited by what it manifests, not contained by the incomplete forms of the manifestation, not tarnished by the imperfections and impurities, the defects and depravations of the surface being. It is an ever-pure flame of the divinity in things and nothing that comes to it, nothing that enters into our experience can pollute its purity or extinguish the flame. This spiritual stuff is immaculate and luminous and, because it is perfectly luminous, it is immediately, intimately, directly aware of truth of being and truth of nature; it is deeply conscious of truth and good and beauty because truth and good and beauty are akin to its own native character, forms of something that is inherent in its own substance. It is aware also of all that contradicts these things, of all that deviates from its own native character, of falsehood and evil and the ugly and the unseemly; but it does not become these things nor is it touched or changed by these opposites of itself which so powerfully affect its outer instrumentation of mind, life and body. For the soul, the permanent being in us, puts forth and uses mind, life and body as its instruments, undergoes the envelopment of their conditions, but it is other and greater than its members.

If the psychic entity had been from the beginning unveiled and known to its ministers, not a secluded King in a screened chamber, the human evolution would have been a rapid soul-outflowering, not the difficult, chequered and disfigured development it now is; but the veil is thick and we know not the secret Light within us, the light in the hidden crypt of the heart's innermost sanctuary. Intimations rise to our surface from the psyche, but our mind does not detect their source; it takes them for its own activities because, before even they come to the surface, they are clothed in mental substance: thus ignorant of their authority, it follows or does not follow them according to its bent or turn at the moment. If the mind obeys the urge of the vital ego, then there is little chance of the psyche at all controlling the nature or manifesting in us something of its secret spiritual stuff and native movement; or, if the mind is over-confident to act in its own smaller light, attached to its own judgment, will and action of knowledge, then also the soul will remain veiled and quiescent and wait for the mind's farther evolution. For the psychic part within is there to support the natural evolution, and the first natural evolution must be the development of body, life and mind, successively, and these must act each in its own kind or together in their ill-assorted partnership in order to grow and have experience and evolve. The soul gathers the essence of all our mental, vital and bodily experience and assimilates it for the farther evolution of our existence in Nature; but this action is occult and not obtruded on the surface. In the early material and vital stages of the evolution of being there is indeed no consciousness of soul; there are psychic activities, but the instrumentation, the form of these activities are vital and physical, – or mental when the mind is active. For even the mind, so long as it is primitive or is developed but still too external, does not recognise their deeper character. It is easy to regard ourselves as physical beings or beings of life or mental beings using life and body and to ignore the existence of the soul altogether: for the only definite idea that we have of the soul is of something that survives the death of our bodies; but what this is we do not know because even if we are conscious sometimes of its presence, we are not normally conscious of its distinct reality nor do we feel clearly its direct action in our nature.

As the evolution proceeds, Nature begins slowly and tentatively to manifest our occult parts; she leads us to look more and more within ourselves or sets out to initiate more clearly recognisable intimations and formations of them on the surface. The soul in us, the psychic principle, has already begun to take secret form; it puts forward and develops a soul-personality, a distinct psychic being to represent it. This psychic being remains still behind the veil in our subliminal part, like the true mental, the true vital or the true or subtle physical being within us: but, like them, it acts on the surface life by the influences and intimations it throws up upon that surface; these form part of the surface aggregate which is the conglomerate effect of the inner influences and upsurgings, the visible formation and superstructure which we ordinarily experience and think of as ourselves. On this ignorant surface we become dimly aware of something that can be called a soul as distinct from mind, life or body; we feel it not only as our mental idea or vague instinct of ourselves, but as a sensible influence in our life and character and action. A certain sensitive feeling for all that is true and good and beautiful, fine and pure and noble, a response to it, a demand for it, a pressure on mind and life to accept and formulate it in our thought, feelings, conduct, character is the most usually recognised, the most general and characteristic, though not the sole sign of this influence of the psyche. Of the man who has not this element in him or does not respond at all to this urge, we say that he has no soul. For it is this influence that we can most easily recognise as a finer or even a diviner part in us and the most powerful for the slow turning towards some aim at perfection in our nature.

But this psychic influence or action does not come up to the surface quite pure or does not remain distinct in its purity; if it did, we would be able to distinguish clearly the soul element in us and follow consciously and fully its dictates. An occult mental and vital and subtle-physical action intervenes, mixes with it, tries to use it and turn it to its own profit, dwarfs its divinity, distorts or diminishes its self-expression, even causes it to deviate and stumble or stains it with the impurity, smallness and error of mind and life and body. After it reaches the surface, thus alloyed and diminished, it is taken hold of by the surface nature in an obscure reception and ignorant formation, and there is or can be by this cause a still further deviation and mixture. A twist is given, a wrong direction is imparted, a wrong application, a wrong formation, an erroneous result of what is in itself pure stuff and action of our spiritual being; a formation of consciousness is accordingly made which is a mixture of the psychic influence and its intimations jumbled with mental ideas and opinions, vital desires and urges, habitual physical tendencies. There coalesce too with the obscured soul-influence the ignorant though well-intentioned efforts of these external parts towards a higher direction; a mental ideation of a very mixed character, often obscure even in its idealism, sometimes even disastrously mistaken, a fervour and passion of the emotional being throwing up its spray and foam of feelings, sentiments, sentimentalisms, a dynamic enthusiasm of the life-parts, eager responses of the physical, the thrills and excitements of nerve and body, – all these influences coalesce in a composite formation which is frequently taken as the soul and its mixed and confused action for the soul-stir, for a psychic development and action or a realised inner influence. The psychic entity is itself free from stain or mixture, but what comes up from it is not protected by that immunity; therefore this confusion becomes possible.

Moreover, the psychic being, the soul-personality in us, does not emerge full-grown and luminous; it evolves, passes through a slow development and formation; its figure of being may be at first indistinct and may afterwards remain for a long time weak and undeveloped, not impure but imperfect: for it rests its formation, its dynamic self-building on the power of soul that has been actually and more or less successfully, against the resistance of the Ignorance and Inconscience, put forth in the evolution upon the surface. Its appearance is the sign of a soul-emergence in Nature, and if that emergence is as yet small and defective, the psychic personality also will be stunted or feeble. It is too, by the obscurity of our consciousness, separated from its inner reality, in imperfect communication with its own source in the depths of the being; for the road is as yet ill-built, easily obstructed, the wires often cut or crowded with communications of another kind and proceeding from another origin: its power to impress what it receives upon the outer instruments is also imperfect; in its penury it has for most things to rely on these instruments and it forms its push to expression and action on their data and not solely on the unerring perceptions of the psychic entity. In these conditions it cannot prevent the true psychic light from being diminished or distorted in the mind into a mere idea or opinion, the psychic feeling in the heart into a fallible emotion or mere sentiment, the psychic will to action in the life-parts into a blind vital enthusiasm or a fervid excitement: it even accepts these mistranslations for want of something better and tries to fulfil itself through them. For it is part of the work of the soul to influence mind and heart and vital being and turn their ideas, feelings, enthusiasms, dynamisms in the direction of what is divine and luminous; but this has to be done at first imperfectly, slowly and with a mixture. As the psychic personality grows stronger, it begins to increase its communion with the psychic entity behind it and improve its communications with the surface: it can transmit its intimations to the mind and heart and life with a greater purity and force; for it is more able to exercise a strong control and react against false mixtures; now more and more it makes itself distinctly felt as a power in the nature. But even so this evolution would be slow and long if left solely to the difficult automatic action of the evolutionary Energy; it is only when man awakes to the knowledge of the soul and feels a need to bring it to the front and make it the master of his life and action that a quicker conscious method of evolution intervenes and a psychic transformation becomes possible.

SRI AUROBINDO

The psychic part of us is something that comes direct from the Divine and is in touch with the Divine. In its origin it is the nucleus pregnant with divine possibilities that supports this lower triple manifestation of mind, life and body. There is this divine element in all living beings, but it stands hidden behind the ordinary consciousness, is not at first developed and, even when developed, is not always or often in the front; it expresses itself, so far as the imperfection of the instruments allows, by their means and under their limitations. It grows in the consciousness by Godward experience, gaining strength every time there is a higher movement in us, and, finally, by the accumulation of these deeper and higher movements, there is developed a psychic individuality, – that which we call usually the psychic being. It is always this psychic being that is the real, though often the secret cause of man's turning to the spiritual life and his greatest help in it. It is therefore that which we have to bring from behind to the front in the yoga.

SRI AUROBINDO

Mother, is the orientation of an individual's life directed by the psychic?

Yes. Absolutely unconsciously for the individual, most of the time; but it is the psychic which organises his existence – only in what may be called the main lines, because for intervening in the details there would have to be a conscious union between the outer being, that is, the vital and physical being, and the psychic being, but usually this does not exist. So externally, in the details... for example, there was someone who in deep perplexity said to me, "Well, if it is the psychic being or rather the Divine in the psychic who directs our life, is it He who decides the number of pieces of sugar I put in my tea-cup?" That was the question, verbatim. So the answer had to be, "No, because it is not a detailed intervention of this kind."

It is as when you push your fist into a heap of iron filings or saw-dust, all the infinitesimal little elements of the iron filings or saw-dust are organised to take on the form of your fist, but they do not do this either deliberately or consciously. It is through the work of the consciousness which pushes that this kind of thing happens. There is no decision that each element is going to be exactly in this place, like that; it is the effect of the energy which has pushed the fist that organises the elements. But that's how it is. There is the psychic consciousness at work in life, organising all the circumstances of your life but not with a deliberate choice of the details....

THE MOTHER

Has the psychic any power?

Power? It is usually the psychic which guides the being. One knows nothing about it because one is not conscious of it but usually it is that which guides the being. If one is very attentive, one becomes aware of it. But the majority of men haven't the least idea of it. For instance, when they have decided, in their outer ignorance, to do something, and instead of their being able to do it, all the circumstances are so organised that they do something else, they start shouting, storming, flying into a rage against fate, saying (that depends on what they believe, their beliefs) that Nature is wicked or their destiny baleful or God unjust, or... no matter what (it depends on what they believe). Whilst most of the time it is just the very circumstance which was most favourable for their inner development. And naturally, if you ask the psychic to help you to fashion a pleasant life for yourself, to earn money, have children who will be the pride of the family, etc., well, the psychic will not help you. But it will create for you all the circumstances necessary to awaken something in you so that the need of union with the Divine may be born in your consciousness. At times you have made fine plans, and if they had succeeded, you would have been more and more encrusted in your outer ignorance, your stupid little ambition and your aimless activity. Whilst if you receive a good shock, and the post you coveted is denied to you, the plan you made is shattered, and you find yourself completely thwarted, then, sometimes this opposition opens to you a door on something truer and deeper. And when you are a little awake and look back, if you are in the least sincere, you say: "Ah! it wasn't I who was right – it was Nature or the divine Grace or my psychic being who did it." It is the psychic being which organised that.

THE MOTHER

III

HIDDEN FORCES AROUND

There is no visible foe, but the unseen
Is round us, forces intangible besiege,
Touches from alien realms, thoughts not our own
Overtake us and compel the erring heart;
Our lives are caught in an ambiguous net.

SRI AUROBINDO
Savitri, Book Six, Canto Two

A grisly company of maladies
Come, licensed lodgers, into man's bodily house,
Purveyors of death and torturers of life.
In the malignant hollows of the world,
In its subconscient cavern-passages
Ambushed they lie waiting their hour to leap,
Surrounding with danger the sieged city of life:
Admitted into the citadel of man's days
They mine his force and maim or suddenly kill.

Ibid.

HIDDEN FORCES AROUND

Outside Suggestions and Vibrations

A suggestion is not one's own thought or feeling, but a thought or feeling that comes from outside, from others, from the general atmosphere or from external Nature, – if it is received, it sticks and acts on the being and is taken to be one's own thought or feeling. If it is recognised as a suggestion, then it can be more easily got rid of.

SRI AUROBINDO

By suggestion I do not mean merely thoughts or words. When the hypnotist says "sleep", it is a suggestion; but when he says nothing, but only puts his silent will to convey sleep or makes movements of his hands over the face, that also is a suggestion.

When a force is thrown on you or a vibration of illness, it carries to the body this suggestion. A wave comes in the body – with a certain vibration in it, the body remembers "cold" or feels the vibrations of a cold and begins to cough or sneeze or to feel chill – the suggestion comes to the mind in the form "I am weak, I don't feel well, I am catching a cold".

SRI AUROBINDO

I have another question about what I told you the other day, when we discussed the distinction between will and "willings". I told you that "willings" – what Sri Aurobindo calls "willings" – are movements arising not

from a higher consciousness coming down into the being
and expressing itself in action, but from impulses or
influences from outside. We reserved the word will to
express what in the individual consciousness is the expression of an order or impulse coming from the truth of
the being, from the truth of the individual – his true being,
his true self, you understand. That we call will. And all the
impulses, actions, movements arising in the being which
are not that, we said were willings. And I told you in fact
that without knowing it or at times even knowing it, you
are moved by influences coming from outside which enter
in without your even being aware of them and arouse in
you what you call the "will" that a certain thing may
happen or another may not, etc.

So I am asked:

> *"What is the nature of these influences from outside?*
> *Could you give us an explanation of their working?"*

Naturally these influences are of very diverse kinds. They
may be studied from a psychological point of view or from
an almost mechanical standpoint, the one usually trans-
lating the other, that is, the mechanical phenomenon
occurs as a sort of result of the psychological one.

In very few people, and even in the very best at very
rare moments in life, does the will of the being express
that deep inner, higher truth.

(*After a silence Mother continues:*) The individual
consciousness extends far beyond the body; we have seen
that even the subtle physical which is yet material compared with the vital being and in certain conditions almost
visible, extends at times considerably beyond the visible

limits of the physical body. This subtle physical is constituted of active vibrations which enter into contact or
mingle with the vibrations of the subtle physical of others,
and this reciprocal contact gives rise to influences –
naturally the most powerful vibrations get the better of
the others. For example, as I have already told you several
times, if you have a thought, this thought clothes itself in
subtle vibrations and becomes an entity which travels and
moves about in the earth-atmosphere in order to realise
itself as best it can, and because it is one among millions,
naturally there is a multiple and involved interaction as a
result of which things don't take place in such a simple and
schematic fashion.

What you call yourself, the individual being enclosed
within the limits of your present consciousness, is constantly penetrated by vibrations of this kind, coming from
outside and very often presenting themselves in the form
of suggestions, in the sense that, apart from a few
exceptions, the action takes place first in the mental field,
then becomes vital, then physical. I want to make it clear
that it is not a question of the pure mind here, but of the
physical mind; for in the physical consciousness itself
there is a mental activity, a vital activity and a purely
material activity, and all that takes place in your physical
consciousness, in your body consciousness and bodily
activity, penetrates first in the form of vibrations of a
mental nature, and so in the form of suggestions. Most of
the time these suggestions enter you without your being in
the least conscious of them; they go in, awaken some sort
of response in you, then spring up in your consciousness as
though they were your own thought, your own will, your
own impulse; but it is only because you are unconscious

of the process of their penetration.

These suggestions are very numerous, manifold, varied, with natures which are very, very different from each other, but they may be classified into three principal orders. First – and they are hardly perceptible to the ordinary consciousness; they become perceptible only to those who have already reflected much, observed much, deeply studied their own being – they are what could be called collective suggestions.

When a being is born upon earth, he is inevitably born in a certain country and a certain environment. Due to his physical parents he is born in a set of social, cultural, national, sometimes religious circumstances, a set of habits of thinking, of understanding, of feeling, conceiving, all sorts of constructions which are at first mental, then become vital habits and finally material modes of being. To put things more clearly, you are born in a certain society or religion, in a particular country, and this society has a collective conception of its own and this nation has a collective conception of its own, this religion has a collective "construction" of its own which is usually very fixed. You are born into it. Naturally, when you are very young, you are altogether unaware of it, but it acts on your formation – that formation, that slow formation through hours and hours, through days and days, experiences added to experiences, which gradually builds up a consciousness. You are underneath it as beneath a bell-glass. It is a kind of construction which covers and in a way protects you, but in other ways limits you considerably. All this you absorb without even being aware of it and this forms the subconscious basis of your own construction. This subconscious basis will act on you throughout your life, if you do not take care to free yourself from it. And to free yourself from it, you must first of all become aware of it; and the first step is the most difficult, for this formation was so subtle, it was made when you were not yet a conscious being, when you had just fallen altogether dazed from another world into this one (*laughing*) and it all happened without your participating in the least in it. Therefore, it does not even occur to you that there could be something to know there, and still less something you must get rid of. And it is quite remarkable that when for some reason or other you do become aware of the hold of this collective suggestion, you realise at the same time that a very assiduous and prolonged labour is necessary in order to get rid of it. But the problem does not end there.

You live surrounded by people. These people them-selves have desires, stray wishes, impulses which are expressed through them and have all kinds of causes, but take in their consciousness an individual form. For example, to put it in very practical terms: you have a father, a mother, brothers, sisters, friends, comrades; each one has his own way of feeling, willing, and all those with whom you are in relation expect something from you, even as you expect something from them. That something they do not always express to you, but it is more or less conscious in their being, and it makes formations. These formations, according to each one's capacity of thought and the strength of his vitality, are more or less powerful, but they have their own little strength which is usually much the same as yours; and so what those around you want, desire, hope or expect from you enters in this way in the form of suggestions very rarely expressed, but which you absorb without resistance and which suddenly awaken within you a similar desire, a similar will, a similar impulse.... This happens from morning to night, and again from night to morning, for these things don't stop while you are sleeping, but on the contrary are very often intensified because your consciousness is no longer awake, watching and protecting you to some extent.

And this is quite common, so common that it is quite natural and so natural that you need special circumstances and most unusual occasions to become aware of it. Naturally, it goes without saying that your own responses, your own impulses, your own wishes have a similar influence on others, and that all this becomes a marvellous mixture in which might is always right!

If that were the end of the problem, one could yet come out of the mess; but there is a complication. This terrestrial world, this human world is constantly invaded by the forces of the neighbouring world, that is, of the vital world, the subtler region beyond the fourfold earth-atmosphere,* and this vital world which is not under the influence of the psychic forces or the psychic consciousness is essentially a world of ill-will, of disorder, disequilibrium, indeed of all the most anti-divine things one could imagine. This vital world is constantly penetrating the physical world, and being much more subtle than the physical, it is very often quite imperceptible except to a few rare individuals. There are entities, beings, wills, various kinds of individualities in that world, who have all kinds of intentions and make use of every opportunity either to amuse themselves if they are small beings or to do harm and create disorder if they are beings with a

---

* Consisting of the four principles: physical, vital, mental and psychic.

greater capacity. And the latter have a very considerable power of penetration and suggestion, and wherever there is the least opening, the least affinity, they rush in, for it is a game which delights them.

Besides, they are very thirsty or hungry for certain human vital vibrations which for them are a rare dish they love to feed upon; and so their game lies in exciting pernicious movements in man so that man may emanate these forces and they be able to feed on them just as they please. All movements of anger, violence, passion, desire, all these things which make you abruptly throw off certain energies from yourself, project them from yourself, are exactly what these entities of the vital world like best, for, as I said, they enjoy them like a sumptuous dish. Now, their tactics are simple: they send you a little suggestion, a little impulse, a small vibration which enters deep into you and through contagion or sympathy awakens in you the vibration necessary to make you throw off the force they want to absorb.

There it is a little easier to recognise the influence, for, if you are the least bit attentive, you become aware of something that has suddenly awakened within you. For example, those who are in the habit of losing their temper, if they have attempted ever so little to control their anger, they will find something coming from outside or rising from below which actually takes hold of their consciousness and arouses anger in them. I don't mean that everybody is capable of this discernment; I am speaking of those who have tried to understand their being and control it. These adverse suggestions are easier to distinguish than, for instance, your response to the will or desire of a being who is of the same nature as yourself, another human being, who consequently acts on you without this giving you a clear impression of something coming from outside: the vibrations are too alike, too similar in their nature, and you have to be much more attentive and have a much sharper discernment to realise that these movements which seem to come out from you are not really yours but come from outside. But with the adverse forces, if you are in the least sincere and observe yourself attentively, you become aware that it is something in the being which is responding to an influence, an impulse, a suggestion, even something at times very concrete, which enters and produces similar vibrations in the being.

There, now. That is the problem.

The remedy?... It is always the same: goodwill, sincerity, insight, patience – oh! an untiring patience and a perseverance which assures you that what you have not succeeded in doing today, you will succeed in doing another time, and makes you go. on trying until you do succeed.

And this brings us back to Sri Aurobindo's sentence: if this control seems to you quite impossible today, well, that means that not only will it be possible, but that it will be realised later.

THE MOTHER

You said that our body can become receptive to forces which are concentrated in certain places or in certain countries.* But can we have this physical sensation

---

* In the preceding talk Mother had described how on her return from Japan she had all of a sudden physically felt the atmosphere of Sri Aurobindo at a distance of two nautical miles from Pondicherry.

*without a preliminary preparation of the conscious-
ness? Or is it truly a spontaneous sensation like heat,
cold or goose-flesh, for example?*

If it were the result of a thought or a will, it would not be
an experience and it would have no value. You understand, I affirm absolutely that any experience that is the
result of a thought or preconceived will has no value from
the spiritual point of view.

*But were you not in a state, so to say, "favourable" to
this sensation?*

There are people who live constantly in a higher consciousness, while others have to make an effort to enter
there. But here it is an altogether different thing; in the
experience I was speaking about, what gave it all its value
was that I was not expecting it at all, not at all. I knew very
well, I had been for a very long time and continuously in
"spiritual" contact, if I may say so, with the atmosphere of
Sri Aurobindo, but I had never thought of the possibility
of a modification in the physical air and I was not
expecting it in the least, and it was this that gave the whole
value to the experience, which came like that, quite
suddenly, just as when one enters a place with another
temperature or another altitude.... I do not know if you
have noticed that the air you breathe is not always the
same, that there are different vibrations in the air of one
country and in the air of another, in the air of one place
and in the air of another. If indeed you are accustomed to
have this perception of the subtle physical, you can say

immediately, "Ah! this air is as in France" or "This is the air of Japan." It is something indefinable like taste or smell. But in this instance it is not that, it is a perception of another sense. It is a physical sense, it is not a vital or mental sense; it is a sense of the physical world, but there are other senses than the five that we usually have at our disposal – there are many others.

In fact, for the physical being – note that I say the physical being – to be fully developed, it must have twelve senses. It is one of these senses which gives you the kind of perception I was speaking of. You cannot say that it is taste, smell, hearing, etc., but it is something which gives you a very precise impression of the difference of quality. And it is very precise, as distinct as seeing black and white, it is truly a sense perception.

THE MOTHER

One lives amidst constant collective suggestions, constantly; for example, I don't know if you have been present at funerals, or if you have been in a house where someone has died – naturally you must observe yourself a little, otherwise you won't notice anything – but if you observe yourself a little, you will see that you had no special reason to feel any sorrow or grief whatever for the passing away of this person; he is a person like many others; this has happened and by a combination of social circumstances you have come to that house. And there, suddenly, without knowing why or how, you feel a strong emotion, a great sorrow, a deep pain, and you ask yourself, "Why am I so unhappy?" It is quite simply the vibrations which have entered you, nothing else.

And I tell you it is easy to observe, for it is an experience I had when I was a little child – and at that time I was not yet doing conscious yoga; perhaps I was doing yoga but not consciously – and I observed it very, very clearly. I told myself, "Surely it is their sorrow I am feeling, for I have no reason to be specially affected by this person's death"; and all of a sudden, tears came to my eyes, I felt as though a lump were in my throat and I wanted to cry, as though I were in great sorrow – I was a small child – and immediately I understood, "Oh! it is their sorrow which has come inside me."

It is the same thing for anger. It is very clear, one receives it suddenly, not even from a person, from the atmosphere – it is there – and then all of a sudden it enters you and usually it gets hold of you from below and then rises up and pushes you, and so off you go. A minute earlier you were not angry, you were quite self-possessed, you had no intention of losing your temper. And this seizes you so strongly that you can't resist – because you are not sufficiently conscious, you let it enter you, and it makes use of you – you... what you call "yourself", that is to say, your body; for apparently (I say apparently) it is something separate from your neighbour's body. But that is only an optical illusion, because in fact all the time there are what may be called particles, even physical particles, like a sort of radiation which comes out of the body and gets mixed with others; and because of this, when one is very sensitive, one can feel things at a distance.

It is said, for instance, that the blind develop such a sensitivity, so delicate a sense-perception, that when they are nearing an object they feel an impact at a distance. But one can quite easily make the experiment. For example, drawing near to someone without making any noise, then bringing one's hand quite close – sensitive people feel it at once. You haven't put your will for them to feel it, you haven't brought in any psychological element, you have only made a purely physical experiment of approaching noiselessly and without being heard – a sensitive person will feel it at once.

That means that the body seems to end there, but it's simply the way our eyes are made. If we had a little more subtle vision, with a little wider range, well, we would see that there is something which comes out, as something comes out from other bodies – and that all this gets mixed up and interacts.

THE MOTHER

Are you able to know, when you are with others, what comes from you and what from the others? To what extent their way of being, their particular vibrations act upon you? You are not aware of this at all. You live in a kind of "approximate" consciousness, half-awake, half-asleep, in something very vague, where you have to grope like this in order to catch things. But do you have a precise, clear, exact notion of what goes on in you, why it goes on in you? And then, this: the vibrations which come to you from outside and those which come from within you? And then, again, what can come from others, changing all this, giving another orientation? You live in a kind of hazy fluidity, certain small things suddenly crystallise in your consciousness, you have just caught them for a moment; and it is just clear enough like that, as though there was a projector, just something passing on the screen and

becoming clear for a second: the next minute everything
has become vague, imprecise, but you are not aware of
this because you have not even asked yourself the question, because you live in this way.

THE MOTHER

Forces of Our Formations

How can human thought create forms?

In the mental world human thought is constantly creating
forms. Human thought is very creative in the mental
world. All the time when you are thinking, you are
creating forms and you send them out in the atmosphere
and they go and do their work. Constantly you are
surrounded by a heap of small formations.

Naturally, there are people who can't even think
clearly. So they form nothing at all except faint eddies.
But people who think clearly are surrounded by a heap of
little forms which, sometimes, go out to do some work in
others; and when one thinks of them again, they return.

And we have instances of people who are troubled by
their own formations, which return constantly as though
to take possession of them, and which they can't get rid of
because they don't know how to undo the formations they
have made. There are more cases of this kind than one
would think. When they have made a particularly strong
formation – for themselves, you see, relatively – this
formation is always tied up with the one who makes it and
returns to knock at the brain to receive forces and ends up
by truly acting as a necessity. It is a whole world to know;

one truly lives in ignorance, one has powers one doesn't know about, so naturally one uses them very badly. One uses them somewhat unconsciously and very badly.

I don't know if you have ever heard of Madame David-Neel who went to Tibet and has written books on Tibet, and who was a Buddhist; and Buddhists – Buddhists of the strictest tradition – do not believe in the Divine, do not believe in his Eternity and do not believe in gods who are truly divine, but they know admirably how to use the mental domain; and Buddhist discipline makes you a good master of the mental instrument and mental domain.

We used to discuss many things and once she told me: "Listen, I made an experiment." (She had studied a bit of Theosophy also.) She said: "I formed a *mahātmā*; with my thought I formed a *mahātmā*." And she knew (this has been proved) that at a given moment mental formations acquire a personal life independent of the fashioner – though they are linked with him – but independent, in the sense that they can have their own will. And so she told me: "Just imagine, I had made my *mahātmā* so well that he became a personality independent of me and constantly came to trouble me! He used to come, scold me for one thing, give me advice for another, and he wanted to direct my life; and I could not succeed in getting rid of him. It was extremely difficult, and I didn't know what to do!"

So I asked her how she tried. She told me how. She said, 'He troubles me a lot, my *mahātmā* is very troublesome. He does not leave me in peace. He disturbs my meditations, he hinders me from working; and yet I know quite well that it is I who created him, and I can't get rid of him!" Then I said, "That's because you don't have the 'trick'...." (*Mother laughs*) And I explained to her what she should do. And the next day – I used to see her almost every day in those days, you see – the next day she came and told me, "Ah, I am freed from my *mahātmā*!" (*Laughter*) She had not *cut* the connection because that's of no use. One must know how to *re-absorb* one's creation, that is the only way. To swallow up again one's formations.

But, you see, in a smaller measure and less perfectly one is making formations all the time. When, for instance, one thinks of somebody quite powerfully, there is a small emanation of mental substance which, instantaneously, goes to this person, you understand, a vibration of your thought which goes and touches his; and if he is receptive, he sees you. He sees you and tells you, "You came last night to see me!" That's because you made a small formation and this formation went and did its work, which was to put you into contact with this person or else to carry a message if you had something special to tell him; and that was done. This happens constantly, but as it is quite a constant and spontaneous phenomenon and done in ignorance, one is not even aware that one does this, one does it automatically.

People who have desires add to the mental formation a kind of small envelope, a vital shell which gives it a still greater reality. These people are usually surrounded by a number of tiny entities which are their own formations, their own mental formations clothed with vital force, which come all the time to strike them to try to make them realise materially the formations they have made.

You have perhaps read the books of Maurice Magre; there are some in the library. He describes this; he had come here, Maurice Magre, and we spoke and he told me that he had always noticed – he was highly sensitive – he had always noticed that people who have sexual desires are surrounded by a kind of small swarm of entities who are somewhat viscous and rather ugly and which torment them constantly, awakening desire in them. He said he had seen this around certain people. It was like being surrounded by a swarm of mosquitoes, yes! But it is more gross, and much uglier still, and it is viscous, it is horrible, and it turns round and round the person and gives him no peace, and it awakens in him the desire that has formed these entities and they batten on it. It is their food. This is absolutely true. His observation was quite correct. His vision was very true. It *is* like that.

But everyone carries around himself the atmosphere of his own desires. So you don't at all require that people should tell you anything; you have only to look and you see around them exactly the state they are in. They may want to give themselves the airs of angels or saints but they can't deceive you, because that thing is there, turning around them. So, just imagine! (*Mother points to all those seated in front of her.*) You see what you are like, how many of you there, all of you here, and each one has his own little world in this way, of mental formations of which some are clothed in vital substance, and all these crawl together, mix with each other, knock against each other. There is a struggle to see which is the strongest, which tries to realise itself, and all this creates an atmosphere indeed!...

THE MOTHER

*When one meditates there are moments when one sees
very unpleasant forms in front of himself for some
days. It begins and later ends. What does it mean?*

Yes, it means probably that instead of meditating in a
silent concentration, one has opened one's consciousness
either in a vital domain or in a not very pleasant mental
domain. That's what it means. It can also mean – it
depends on the degree of development one has reached –
it can mean in certain cases, when one is master of one's
concentration and knows where one goes – still this
already requires a fairly great discipline – it may be that it
is a particular attack of adverse forces, of bad wills,
coming either from certain beings or from certain domains; but it is not necessarily attacks; it can simply be
that one has opened one's consciousness in a place that's
not very desirable or else sometimes, often, that one had
in himself a number of movements of the vital and the
mind which were not very desirable, and when one enters
the silence of meditation or that kind of passive attitude of
expectation of something which is going to happen, all
these vibrations which have gone out of him come back to
him in their real appearance which is not very pleasant.
This happens often: one had bad feelings, not positively
wicked but still things which are not desirable, bad
thoughts, movements of dissatisfaction, revolt or impa-
tience, or a lack of contentment or... you see, one may be
angry with somebody, even in thought, no need of
speaking... things like that. When one is quiet and tries to
be still so as to have an experience, all these things come
back to him in their true form, that is, not very pleasant
forms: very ugly, forms which are at times very ugly. I

think that I have already told you this several times: it's something that happens frequently if you don't control your thoughts and your vital reactions and if someone has displeased you for some reason or other, if that person has done or said something which you do not like, and you consider him hostile and so the spontaneous reaction is to want to punish him in some way or other or if one is still more primitive – if I may say so – to want to take vengeance or hope that something bad will happen to him.

However, it may even come very spontaneously, a violent reaction, like that, then you don't think about it any more. But now, at night, when you are asleep, ninety-nine times out of a hundred, in a case like this, the person in question comes to you with an extreme violence, either to kill you or to make you ill, as though he wished you as much harm as possible, and then in your ignorance you say, "Well, I was quite right to be angry with him." But it is quite simply your own formation which returns to you, nothing else but that. The person has nothing to do with it – he is quite innocent in the affair. This is a phenomenon which occurs very often, I mean for people who have movements of rancour or anger or violence; and they always see in a dream of this kind the justification of their movements – whereas it is only a very striking image of their own feelings. For the formation returns upon one in this way.

THE MOTHER

Forces of Illness and Accident

The suggestions that create illness or unhealthy conditions

of the physical being come usually through the subconscient – for a great part of the physical being, the most material part, is subconscient, i.e. to say, it has an obscure consciousness of its own but so obscure and shut up in itself that the mind does not know its movements or what is going on there. But all the same it is a consciousness and can receive suggestions from Forces outside, just as the mind and vital do. If it were not so, there would not be any possibility of opening it to the Force and the Force curing it; for without this consciousness in it it would not be able to respond. In Europe and America there are many people now who recognise this fact and treat their illnesses by making conscious mental suggestions to the body which counteract the obscure secret suggestions of illness in the subconscient. There was a famous Doctor in France who cured thousands of people by making them persistently put such counter-suggestions upon the body. That proves that illness has not a purely material cause, but is due to a disturbance of the secret consciousness in the body.

SRI AUROBINDO

That is how illnesses try to come from one person to another – they attack, by a suggestion like this or otherwise, the nervous being and try to come in. Even if the illness is not contagious, this often happens, but it comes more easily in contagious illnesses. The suggestion or touch has to be thrown off at once.

There is a sort of protection round the body which we call the nervous envelope – if this remains strong and refuses entrance to the illness force, then one can remain well even in the midst of plague or other epidemics – if the envelope is pierced or weak, then the illness can come in.

What you felt attacked was not really the physical body, but this nervous envelope and the nervous body (*prāṇa-koṣa*) of which it is an extension or cover.

SRI AUROBINDO

They [the subtle forces of illness] first weaken or break through the nervous envelope, the aura. If that is strong and whole, a thousand million germs will not be able to do anything to you. The envelope pierced, they attack the subconscient mind in the body, sometimes also the vital mind or mind proper – prepare the illness by fear or thought of illness. The doctors themselves say that in influenza or cholera in the Far East 90 p.c. get ill through fear. Nothing to take away the resistance like fear. But still the subconscient is the main thing.

If the contrary Force is strong in the body one can move in the midst of plague and cholera and never get contaminated.

SRI AUROBINDO

Attacks of illness are attacks of the lower nature or of adverse forces taking advantage of some weakness, opening or response in the nature, – like all other things that come and have got to be thrown away, they come from outside. If one can feel them so coming and get the strength and the habit to throw them away before they can enter the body, then one can remain free from illness. Even when the attack seems to rise from within, that means only that it has not been detected before it entered the subconscient; once in the subconscient, the force that brought it rouses it from there sooner or later and it invades the system. When you feel it just after it has entered, it is because though it came direct and not through the subconscient, yet you could not detect it while it was still outside. Very often it arrives like that frontally or more often tangentially from the side direct, forcing its way through the subtle vital envelope which is our main armour of defence, but it can be stopped there in the envelope itself before it penetrates the material body. Then one may feel some effect, e.g., feverishness or a tendency to cold, but there is not the full invasion of the malady. If it can be stopped earlier or if the vital envelope of itself resists and remains strong, vigorous and intact, then there is no illness; the attack produces no physical effect and leaves no traces.

SRI AUROBINDO

When Sri Aurobindo says that illness comes from outside, what exactly is it that comes?

It is a kind of vibration made up of a mental suggestion, a vital force of disorder and certain physical elements which are the materialisation of the mental suggestion and the vital vibration. And these physical elements can be what we have agreed to call germs, microbes, this and that and many other things.

It may be accompanied by a sensation, may be accompanied by a taste, also by a smell, if one has very developed subtle senses. There are these formations of

illness which give a special taste to the air, a special smell
or a slight special sensation.

People have many senses which are asleep. They are
terribly tamasic. If all the senses they possess were awake,
there are many things they would perceive, which can just
pass by without anyone suspecting anything.

For example, many people have a certain kind of
influenza at the moment. It is very wide-spread. Well,
when it comes close, it has a special taste, a special smell,
and it brings you a certain contact (naturally not like a
blow), something a little more subtle, a certain contact,
exactly as when you pass your hand over something,
backwards over some material... You have never done
that? The material has a grain, you know; when you pass
your hand in the right direction or when you pass it like
this (*gesture*), well, it makes you... it is something that
passes over your skin, like this, backwards. But naturally,
I can tell you, it doesn't come like a staggering blow. It is
very subtle but very clear. So if you see that, you can very
easily...

Besides, there is always a way of isolating oneself by an
atmosphere of protection, if one knows how to have an
extremely quiet vibration, so quiet that it makes almost a
kind of wall around you. – But all the time, all the time
one is vibrating in response to vibrations which come from
outside. If you become aware of this, all the time there is
something which does this (*gesture*), like this, like this,
like this (*gestures*), which responds to all the vibrations
coming from outside. You are never in an absolutely quiet
atmosphere which emanates from you, that is, which
comes from inside outward (not something which comes
from outside within), something which is like an envelope

around you, very quiet, like this – and you can go anywhere at all and these vibrations which come from outside do not begin to do this (*gesture*) around your atmosphere.

If you could see that kind of dance, the dance of vibrations which is there around you all the time, you would see, would understand well what I mean.

For example, in a game, when you play, it is like this (*gesture*), and then it is like the vibrations of a point, it goes on increasing, increasing and increasing until suddenly, crash!... an accident. And it is a collective atmosphere like that; we come and see it, you are in the midst of a game – basketball or football or any other – we feel it, see it, it produces a kind of smoke around you (those vapours of heat which come at times, something like that), and then it takes on a vibration like that, like that, more and more, more and more, more and more until suddenly the equilibrium is broken: someone breaks his leg, falls down, is hit on the mouth by a ball, etc. And one can foretell beforehand that this is going to happen when it is like that. But nobody is aware of it.

Yet, even in less serious cases, each one of you individually has around him something which instead of being this very individual and very calm envelope which protects you from all that you don't want to receive... I mean, your receptivity becomes deliberate and conscious, otherwise you do not receive; and it is only when you have this conscious extremely calm atmosphere, and as I say, when it comes from within (it is not something that comes from outside), it is only when it's like this that you can go with impunity into life, that is, among others and in all the circumstances of every minute...

Otherwise if there is something bad to be caught, for example, anger, fear, an illness, some uneasiness, you are sure to catch it. As soon as it starts doing this (*gesture*), it is as though you called all similar vibrations to come and get hold of you.

What is to be wondered at is the unconsciousness with which men go through life; they don't know how to live, there's not one in a million who knows how to live, and they live like that somehow or other, limping along....

THE MOTHER

Accidents are due to many things; in fact they are the result of a conflict of the forces in Nature, a conflict between the forces of growth and progress and the forces of destruction. When there is an accident, an accident that has lasting results, it is always the result of a more or less partial victory of the adverse forces, that is, of the forces of disintegration, disorganisation.

THE MOTHER

IV

COSMIC AND UNIVERSAL FORCES

Awakened to the lines that Nature hides,
Attuned to her movements that exceed our ken,
He grew one with a covert universe.
His grasp surprised her mightiest energies' springs;
He spoke with the unknown Guardians of the worlds,
Forms he descried our mortal eyes see not.
His wide eyes bodied viewless entities,
He saw the cosmic forces at their work
And felt the occult impulse behind man's will.

SRI AUROBINDO
Savitri, Book One, Canto Three

COSMIC AND UNIVERSAL FORCES

Nature and Action of Universal Forces

Universal forces means all forces good or bad, favourable or hostile, of light and darkness that move in the cosmos.

SRI AUROBINDO

They [the cosmic forces] act on everyone, according to the person's nature – and his will and consciousness.

SRI AUROBINDO

These [impersonal forces of the world] we know only by their results, by the little that we can seize of their visible action and consequence. Among them it is mostly the physical world-forces of which we have some knowledge, but we live constantly in the midst of a whirl of unseen mind-forces and life-forces of which we know nothing, we are not even aware of their existence. To all this unseen movement and action the subliminal inner consciousness can open our awareness, for it has a knowledge of it by direct contact, by inner vision, by a psychic sensitiveness; but at present it can only enlighten our obtuse super-ficiality and outwardness by unexplained warnings, pre-monitions, attractions and repulsions, ideas, suggestions, obscure intuitions, the little it can get through imperfectly to the surface. The inner being not only contacts directly and concretely the immediate motive and movement of these universal forces and feels the results of their present action, but it can to a certain extent forecast or see ahead their further action; there is a greater power in our subliminal parts to overcome the time barrier, to have the sense or feel the vibration of coming events, of distant happenings, even to look into the future. It is true that this knowledge proper to the subliminal being is not complete; for it is a mixture of knowledge and ignorance and it is capable of erroneous as well as of true perception.

SRI AUROBINDO

... they [cosmic forces] move in masses, waves, currents constantly constituting and reconstituting beings and objects, movements and happenings, entering into them, passing through them, forming themselves in them, throwing themselves out from them on other beings and objects. Each natural individual is a receptacle of these cosmic forces and a dynamo for their propagation; there passes from each to each a constant stream of mental and vital energies, and these run too in cosmic waves and currents no less than the forces of physical Nature. All this action is veiled from our surface mind's direct sense and knowledge, but it is known and felt by the inner being, though only through a direct contact; when the being enters into the cosmic consciousness, it is still more widely, inclusively, intimately aware of this play of cosmic forces.

SRI AUROBINDO

Each man has his own personal consciousness entrenched in his body and gets into touch with his surroundings only through his body and senses and the mind using the senses.

Yet all the time the universal forces are pouring into him without his knowing it. He is aware only of thoughts, feelings, etc., that rise to the surface and these he takes for his own. Really they come from outside in mind waves, vital waves, waves of feeling and sensation, etc., which take particular form in him and rise to the surface after they have got inside.

But they do not get into his body at once. He carries about with him an environmental consciousness (called by the Theosophists the Aura) into which they first enter. If you can become conscious of this environmental self of yours, then you can catch the thought, passion, suggestion or force of illness and prevent it from entering into you. If things in you are thrown out, they often do not go altogether but take refuge in this environmental atmosphere and from there they try to get in again. Or they go to a distance outside but linger on the outskirts or even perhaps far off, waiting till they get an opportunity to attempt entrance.

SRI AUROBINDO

The universal forces act very often through the subconscient – especially when the force they send is something the person has been in the habit of obeying and of which the seeds, impressions, "complexes" are strongly rooted in the subconscient – or, even if that is no longer the case, of which there is a memory still in the subconscient.

SRI AUROBINDO

The forces are conscious. There are besides individualised

beings who represent the forces or use them. The wall between consciousness and force, impersonality and personality becomes much thinner when one goes behind the veil of matter. If one looks at a working from the side of impersonal force one sees a force or energy at work acting for a purpose or with a result, if one looks from the side of being one sees a being possessing, guiding and using or else representative of and used by a conscious force as its instrument of specialised action and expression. You speak of the wave, but in modern science it has been found that if you look at the movement of energy, it appears on one side to be a wave and act as a wave, on the other as a mass of particles and to act as a mass of particles each acting in its own way. It is somewhat the same principle here.

SRI AUROBINDO

Is time only subjective or it is something concrete like a personality?

All forces are personal; all things in Nature are personal. But if we consider them as impersonal things, our relation with them is impersonal.

Take for instance what has just happened. If you are a meteorologist and have calculated all the wind-currents and all that, and say, "Given that this has happened, that will happen, and there will be so many days of rain, and all that." So this is a force for you, which we are compelled to call a force of Nature, and you can do nothing about it except look on quietly and wait for the number of days to pass. But if it happens that you have this personal relation with the little conscious entities which are behind the wind, behind the storm, behind the rain, the thunder, behind all these so-called forces of Nature, which are forces and personal forces, if you have a personal relation with them and can create a kind of friendship through this relation, instead of considering them as enemies and inexorable mechanisms which you have to put up with without being able to do anything, perhaps you could manage to establish a slightly more friendly relation and have an influence over them and ask them: "Why do you feel like blowing and making the rain fall, why don't you do it elsewhere?"

And with my own eyes I have seen... I have seen this here, seen it in France, seen it in Algeria... the rain falling at a particular, altogether fixed place, and it was exactly a place where it absolutely needed to rain, because it was dry and there was a field which needed watering, and at another place there was... at a distance from here to the end of the hall, at the other place there was a small sunlit spot, everything was dry, because to have the sun there was necessary. Naturally, if you seek the scientific point of view, they will explain this to you very scientifically. But I indeed have seen it as the result of an intervention... someone who knew how to ask it and obtained it.

In Algeria I saw not a few things like that, very interesting ones. And there, just because there was a certain atmosphere of a little more real knowledge it could be said, there were little entities, as for example entities which handled snow, you see, which produced snow, and which could come, enter a room and tell someone, "Now snow should fall here!" (It had never snowed in that country, never.) "Snow! you are joking. So near the

Sahara it is going to snow?" "It must, because they have planted fir trees on the mountain, and when we see fir trees, we come. The fir trees are there to call us; so we come." And so, you see, there was a discussion, and the little being went away with the permission to bring snow, and when it had gone, there was a little pool of snow water on the floor, melted snow which had turned into water. It was physical... and the mountain was covered with snow. In Algeria! It is *very near* the Sahara, you go down a few kilometres and you are at the Sahara. Someone had playfully covered all the hills with fir trees. "The fir tree belongs to cold countries. Why do you call us? We are coming." All this is a true story, it is not an invention.

All depends on your relation. This too, it is quite possible the meteorologist scholars would have been able to explain, I know nothing about it, they explain everything one wants.

THE MOTHER

There are forces, and subliminal experience seems to show that there are supraphysical beings embodying those forces, that are attached in their root-nature to ignorance, to darkness of consciousness, to misuse of force, to perversity of delight, to all the causes and consequences of the things that we call evil. These powers, beings or forces are active to impose their adverse constructions upon terrestrial creatures; eager to maintain their reign in the manifestation, they oppose the increase of light and truth and good and, still more, are antagonistic to the progress of the soul towards a divine consciousness and divine existence. It is this feature of existence that we see figured in the tradition of the conflict between the Powers of Light and Darkness, Good and Evil, cosmic Harmony and cosmic Anarchy, a tradition universal in ancient myth and in religion and common to all systems of occult knowledge.

The theory of this traditional knowledge is perfectly rational and verifiable by inner experience, and it imposes itself if we admit the supraphysical and do not cabin ourselves in the acceptation of material being as the only reality. As there is a cosmic Self and Spirit pervading and upholding the universe and its beings, so too there is a cosmic Force that moves all things, and on this original cosmic Force depend and act many cosmic Forces that are its powers or arise as forms of its universal action. Whatever is formulated in the universe has a Force or Forces that support it, seek to fulfil or further it, find their foundation in its functioning, their account of success in its success and growth and domination, their self-fulfilment or their prolongation of being in its victory or survival. As there are Powers of Knowledge or Forces of the Light, so there are Powers of Ignorance and tenebrous Forces of the Darkness whose work is to prolong the reign of Ignorance and Inconscience. As there are Forces of Truth, so there are Forces that live by the Falsehood and support it and work for its victory; as there are powers whose life is intimately bound up with the existence, the idea and the impulse of Good, so there are Forces whose life is bound up with the existence and the idea and the impulse of Evil. It is this truth of the cosmic Invisible that was symbolised in the ancient belief of a struggle between the powers of Light and Darkness, Good and Evil for the possession of the world and the government of the life of

man; – this was the significance of the contest between the
Vedic Gods and their opponents, sons of Darkness and
Division, figured in a later tradition as Titan and Giant
and Demon, Asura, Rakshasa, Pisacha; the same tradition is found in the Zoroastrian Double Principle and the
later Semitic opposition of God and his Angels on the one
side and Satan and his hosts on the other, – invisible
Personalities and Powers that draw man to the divine
Light and Truth and Good or lure him into subjection to
the undivine principle of Darkness and Falsehood and
Evil. Modern thought is aware of no invisible forces other
than those revealed or constructed by Science; it does not
believe that Nature is capable of creating any other beings
than those around us in the physical world, men, beasts,
birds, reptiles, fishes, insects, germs and animalculae. But
if there are invisible cosmic forces physical in their nature
that act upon the body of inanimate objects, there is no
valid reason why there should not be invisible cosmic
forces mental and vital in their nature that act upon his
mind and his life-force. And if Mind and Life, impersonal
forces, form conscious beings or use persons to embody
them in physical forms and in a physical world and can act
upon Matter and through Matter, it is not impossible that
on their own planes they should form conscious beings
whose subtler substance is invisible to us or that they
should be able to act from those planes on beings in
physical Nature. Whatever reality or mythical unreality
we may attach to the traditional figures of past human
belief or experience, they would then be representations
of things that are true in principle. In that case the first
source of good and evil would be not in terrestrial life or in
the evolution from the Inconscience, but in Life itself,

their source would be supraphysical and they would be reflected here from a larger supraphysical Nature.

This is certain that when we go back into ourselves very deep away from the surface appearance, we find that the mind, heart and sensational being of man are moved by forces not under his own control and that he can become an instrument in the hands of Energies of a cosmic character without knowing the origin of his actions. It is by stepping back from the physical surface into his inner being and subliminal consciousness that he becomes directly aware of them and is able to know directly and deal with their action upon him. He grows aware of interventions which seek to lead him in one direction or another, of suggestions and impulsions which had disguised themselves as original movements of his own mind and against which he had to battle. He can realise that he is not a conscious creature inexplicably produced in an unconscious world out of a seed of inconscient Matter and moving about in an obscure self-ignorance, but an embodied soul through whose action cosmic Nature is seeking to fulfil itself, the living ground of a vast debate between a darkness of Ignorance out of which it emerges here and a light of Knowledge which is growing upwards towards an unforeseen termination. The Forces which seek to move him, and among them the Forces of good and evil, present themselves as powers of universal Nature; but they seem to belong not only to the physical universe, but to planes of Life and Mind beyond it.

The first thing that we have to note of importance to the problem preoccupying us is that these Forces in their action seem often to surpass the measures of human relativity; they are in their larger action superhuman, divine, titanic or demoniac, but they may create their formations in him in large or in little, in his greatness or his smallness, they may seize and drive him at moments or for periods, they may influence his impulses or his acts or possess his whole nature. If that possession happens, he may himself be pushed to an excess of the normal humanity of good or evil; especially the evil takes forms which shock the sense of human measure, exceed the bounds of human personality, approach the gigantic, the inordinate, the immeasurable.

SRI AUROBINDO

Universal Vital Force

Sweet Mother, how can one draw on "the universal vital Force"?

One can do it in many ways.

First of all, you must know that it exists and that one can enter into contact with it. Secondly, you must try to make this contact, to feel it circulating everywhere, through everything, in all persons and all circumstances; to have this experience, for example, when you are in the countryside among trees, to see it circulating in the whole of Nature, in trees and things, and then commune with it, feel yourself close to it, and each time you want to deal with it, recall that impression you had and try to enter into contact.

Some people discover that with certain movements, certain gestures, certain activities, they enter into contact more closely. I knew people who gesticulated while walking... this truly gave them the impression that they were in contact – certain gestures they made while walking... But children do this spontaneously: when they give themselves completely in their games, running, playing, jumping, shouting; when they spend all their energies like that, they give themselves entirely, and in the joy of playing and moving and running they put themselves in contact with this universal vital force; they don't know it, but they spend their vital force in a contact with the universal vital force and that is why they can run without really feeling very tired, except after a very long time. That is, they spend so much that if they were not in contact with the universal force, they would be absolutely exhausted, immediately. And that is why, besides, they grow up; it is also because they receive more than they spend; they know how to receive more than they spend. And this does not correspond to any knowledge. It is a natural, spontaneous movement. It is the movement... a movement of joy in what they are doing – of joyful expenditure. One can do many things with that.

I knew young people who had always lived in cities – in a city and in those little rooms one has in the big cities in which everyone is huddled. Now, they had come to spend their holidays in the countryside, in the south of France, and there the sun is hot, naturally not as here but all the same it is very hot (when we compare the sun of the Mediterranean coasts with that of Paris, for example, it truly makes a difference), and so, when they walked around the countryside the first few days they really began to get a terrible headache and to feel absolutely uneasy because of the sun; but they suddenly thought: "Why, if we make friends with the sun it won't harm us any more!"

And they began to make a kind of inner effort of friendship and trust in the sun, and when they were out in the sun, instead of trying to bend double and tell themselves, "Oh! how hot it is, how it burns!", they said, "Oh, how full of force and joy and love the sun is!" etc., they opened themselves like this (*gesture*), and not only did they not suffer any longer but they felt so strong afterwards that they went round telling everyone who said "It is hot" – telling them "Do as we do, you will see how good it is." And they could remain for hours in the full sun, bareheaded and without feeling any discomfort. It is the same principle.

It is the same principle. They linked themselves to the universal vital force which is in the sun and received this force which took away all that was unpleasant to them.

When one is in the countryside, when one walks under the trees and feels so close to Nature, to the trees, the sky, all the leaves, all the branches, all the herbs, when one feels a great friendship with these things and breathes that air which is so good, perfumed with all the plants, then one opens oneself, and by opening oneself communes with the universal forces. And for all things it is like that.

Can one do the same thing when it is cold?

Yes, I think so. I think one can always do the same thing in all cases.

The sun is a very powerful symbol in the organisation of Nature. So it is not altogether the same thing; it possesses in itself an extraordinary condensation of energy. Cold seems to me a more negative thing: it is an absence of something. But in any case, if one knows how to enter the rhythm of the movements of Nature, one avoids many discomforts. What makes men suffer, what disturbs the balance of the body is a narrowness, it is always a narrowness. It happens because one is shut up in limits, and so there is, as Sri Aurobindo writes here, a force which presses too strongly for these limits – it upsets everything.

THE MOTHER

On what do our physical reserves depend, Mother?

Physical reserves? You mean the reserve of energy?

Yes.

It depends on the capacity to receive the universal vital force; because in fact, through food also it is these vital forces one receives but one receives them from below. But in order to have reserves you must know how to receive the universal vital forces constantly and to have a kind of balance in the being which prevents you from spending more than you have.

A proportion has to be kept between the receptivity and the expenditure. It is a kind of harmony in the being which must be established. Only, some people have an almost instinctive power of attracting towards them the vital forces or absorbing them – the universal vital forces, I mean – and so they make up their expense as they go along spending. These people can produce much more than others. Some of them, in certain conditions like sleep or a kind of repose or relaxation, can accumulate forces and later they exhaust them, so to say, in their activities and they must yet once again charge the battery afterwards – this is already a much less favourable condition.

Some people don't know how to receive the forces at all. These live on the energies concentrated in the body – for there is some concentrated energy in all the cells of the body. They live upon that, but after some time, they are drained out completely if they don't know how to recuperate; when they have spent all the energies which were concentrated inside them either they fall ill or they never recuperate them. So this cannot last very long; it lasts the average lifetime of human beings, and yet, at the end of a certain number of years they are no longer able to make the same effort or to produce as much, or above all to make any progress.

But those who know instinctively or who have learnt to receive and accumulate the universal vital forces, these can last almost indefinitely. The wear and tear is very little, especially if they know how to do it and do it with knowledge and method; then here it can reach a certain degree of perfection.

When one knows, sometimes just two or three minutes are sufficient to recuperate the energies spent over a long period. Only, one must know how to do it.

But those who draw back upon themselves, who turn and double up on themselves, cannot do this. One must live all the time in a very vast and very expansive consciousness (I don't know if you understand the word, it means something which extends very homogeneously and quietly, as when the tide is at its height and the water spreads like that, quietly – that's the impression). The vital must be like that – then one is open to the universal forces. But if, for example, one has the very bad habit of exchanging vital forces with one's fellowmen, then one loses the capacity altogether. So unless one is in relation with someone, one receives nothing at all. But naturally if you receive forces through others, you receive at the same time all the difficulties of the other person, perhaps sometimes his qualities also, but these are less contagious. This indeed is something that shuts you up most.

Some people... unless they have more or less social relations with others, relations of friendship, conversing... and then it goes still farther... they don't receive any forces; and this is how they receive them. But this always makes a soup. The forces one receives are already half digested, in any case they don't have their primal purity, and this affects your own capacity.

But when one has this capacity in his own consciousness – for example, you go for a walk and come to a place which is somewhat vast, like the seashore or like a great plain or the summit of a mountain, a place where the horizon is fairly vast, then if you have this kind of physical instinct which suddenly makes you as vast as the horizon, you have a sense of infinity, immensity; and the vaster you become, the quieter and more peaceful you become.

It is enough for you to have a contact with Nature like that.

There are many other means, but this one is very spontaneous. There is also... when you see something very beautiful you can have the same thing: a kind of inner joy and an opening to the forces, and so this widens you and fills you at the same time. There are many means but usually one does not use them. Naturally, if you enter into contemplation and aspire for a higher life and call down the forces from above, this recuperates your energies more than anything else. But there are numerous methods.

THE MOTHER

Sweet Mother, do the universal vital forces have any limits?

I don't think that forces have a limit, because in comparison with us they are certainly unlimited. But it's our capacity of reception that is limited. We cannot absorb them beyond a certain measure, and then we must keep a balance between the expenditure and the capacity to receive. If one spends suddenly in a kind of impulse – for example, in an impulsive movement – if one spends much more than one has received, one needs a brief moment of concentration, calm, receptivity to absorb universal forces. You must put yourself in a certain condition to receive them; and then, they last for a certain time, and once you have spent them you must begin again to receive them. It is in this sense that there are limits. It isn't the forces that are limited, it is the receptivity.

Each person has a different receptivity. No two receptivities are the same in quality and quantity, but specially in quality. One enters into contact with very pure, very intense forces – what could be already called converted forces, that is, universal vital forces which are in contact with the Divine and not only receive the Divine but aspire to receive Him. So if you absorb these forces it gives you a great strength for progress. It is in this that the quality is much more important. And for the quality of the universal vital forces, it depends naturally a great deal on what one is, but also much on what one does.

If one uses these forces for a purely selfish action of a base kind, well, one makes it almost totally impossible for himself to receive any new ones of as fine a quality. All depends on the utilisation of the forces one receives. If, on the other hand, you use them to make progress, to perfect yourself, it gives you... it increases your capacity of receiving enormously, and the next time you can have a lot more. All depends (in any case, principally) on the use made of them. There are people, for instance, who are short-tempered by nature and haven't succeeded in controlling their anger. Well, if with an aspiration or by some method or other they have managed to receive some higher vital forces, instead of this calming their irritation or anger... because they have no self-control it increases their anger, that is, their irritability, their movement of violence is full of a greater force, a greater energy, and becomes much more violent. So it is well said that to be in contact with universal forces does not make one progress. But this is because they make a bad use of them. Yet naturally in the long run, this bad use diminishes the capacity of receiving; but it takes time, it is not immediate. So it is very important to put yourself in a good condition to receive the higher forces and not the lower ones, and secondly, when you have received them use them for the best thing possible, in order to prepare yourself to receive those which are of a higher quality. But if you open yourself, receive the forces and afterwards, being satisfied with having received them you let yourself fall into all the ordinary movements, well, you close the door and the force no longer returns.

THE MOTHER

V
OCCULT FORCES

In a mist of secrecy wrapping the world-scene
The little deities of Time's nether act
Who work remote from Heaven's controlling eye,
Plotted, unknown to the creatures whom they move,
The small conspiracies of this petty reign
Amused with the small contrivings, the brief hopes
And little eager steps and little ways
And reptile wallowings in the dark and dust,
And the crouch and ignominy of creeping life.
A trepidant and motley multitude,
A strange pell-mell of magic artisans
Was seen moulding the plastic clay of life,
An elfin brood, an elemental kind.
Astonished by the unaccustomed glow,
As if immanent in the shadows started up
Imps with wry limbs and carved beast visages,
Sprite prompters goblin-wizened or faery-small,
And genii fairer but unsouled and poor
And fallen beings, their heavenly portion lost,
And errant divinities trapped in Time's dust.

SRI AUROBINDO
Savitri, Book Two, Canto Five

OCCULT FORCES

Occultism – Science of Hidden Forces

Occultism is associated in popular idea with magic and magical formulae and a supposed mechanism of the supernatural. But this is only one side, nor is it altogether a superstition as is vainly imagined by those who have not looked deeply or at all at this covert side of secret Nature-Force or experimented with its possibilities. Formulas and their application, a mechanisation of latent forces, can be astonishingly effective in the occult use of mind-power and life-power just as it is in physical Science, but this is only a subordinate method and a limited direction. For mind and life forces are plastic, subtle and variable in their action and have not the material rigidity; they need a subtle and plastic intuition in the knowledge of them, in the interpretation of their action and process and in their application, – even in the interpretation and action of their established formulas. An overstress on mechanisation and rigid formulation is likely to result in sterilisation or formalised limitation of knowledge and, on the pragmatic side, to much error, ignorant convention, misuse and failure. Now that we are outgrowing the superstition of the sole truth of Matter, a swing backward towards the old occultism and to new formulations, as well as to a scientific investigation of the still hidden secrets and powers of Mind and a close study of psychic and abnormal or supernormal psychological phenomena, is possible and, in parts, already visible. But if it is to fulfil itself, the true foundation, the true aim and direction, the necessary restrictions and precautions of this line of inquiry have to be rediscovered; its most important aim must be the discovery of the hidden truths and powers of the mind-force and the life-power and the greater forces of the concealed spirit. Occult science is, essentially, the science of the subliminal, the subliminal in ourselves and the subliminal in world-nature, and of all that is in connection with the subliminal, including the subconscient and the superconscient, and the use of it as part of self-knowledge and world-knowledge and for the right dynamisation of that knowledge.

SRI AUROBINDO

These extraordinary occurrences which go outside the ordinary course of physical Nature, happen frequently in India and are not unknown elsewhere; they are akin to what is called poltergeist phenomena in Europe. Scientists do not speak or think about such supernormal happenings except to pooh-pooh them or to prove that they are simply the tricks of children simulating supernatural manifestations.

Scientific laws only give a schematic account of material process of Nature – as a valid scheme they can be used for reproducing or extending at will a material process, but obviously they cannot give an account of the thing itself. Water, for instance, is not merely so much oxygen and hydrogen put together – the combination is simply a process or device for enabling the materialisation of a new thing called water; what that new thing really is, is quite another matter. In fact, there are different planes of substance, gross, subtle and more subtle going back to what is called causal (Karana) substance. What is more gross can be reduced to the subtle state and the subtle brought into the gross state; that accounts for dematerialisation and rematerialisation. These are occult processes and are vulgarly regarded as magic. Ordinarily the magician knows nothing of the why and wherefore of what he is doing, he has simply learned the formula of process or else controls elemental beings of the subtler states (planes or worlds) who do the thing for him. The Tibetans indulge widely in occult processes; if you see the books of Madame David Neel who has lived in Tibet you will get an idea of their expertness in these things. But also the Tibetan Lamas know something of the laws of occult (mental and vital) energy and how it can be made to act on physical things. That is something which goes beyond mere magic. The direct power of mind-force or life-force upon Matter can be extended to an almost illimitable degree. It must be remembered that Energy is fundamentally one in all the planes, only taking more and more dense forms, so there is nothing *a priori* impossible in mind-energy or life-energy acting directly on material energy and substance; if they do, they can make a material object do things or rather can do things with a material object which would be to that object in its ordinary poise or "law" unhabitual and therefore apparently impossible.

SRI AUROBINDO

... you must not mix up magic with occultism.

Occultism is a science and it is the knowledge of invisible forces and the capacity to handle them, as one has the capacity of handling material forces if one has studied them scientifically.

Magic: these are different kinds of processes which were fixed probably by people who had a certain knowledge, and still more a certain power of vital formation. These things can be learnt without having any special capacity, that is, someone who has no inner power can learn this as he learns chemistry, for example, or mathematics. It is one of the things which are learnt like that, it is not a thing one acquires. So it doesn't itself carry any special virtues except the same kind of qualities as those one learns through chemical manipulations. You may reproduce these manipulations, but if you are an intelligent and capable being, you can by the help of these manipulations obtain an interesting and useful result, and in any case, be sheltered from all danger; whereas if you are an idiot, misfortunes may come to you. It is something similar.

With the help of magical formulas one may produce a certain result, but this result is necessarily limited and has no particular interest for those who, through their inner development, spontaneously receive powers of which they have a higher knowledge, not a mechanical one. It is not for someone who is truly a yogi; it has no interest except that of curiosity. It is interesting only for people who are precisely not yogis and who want to have certain powers which, in fact, they have in a very limited way – it is always limited.

What is special about it is that it has a direct action upon matter; while usually, apart from some rare exceptions, with people who have spiritual powers, yogic powers, it acts through the intermediary of the mental forces usually – either spiritual or mental forces – sometimes of the vital forces (more rarely), but not directly upon matter, except naturally with those who have done yoga in matter, but these are exceptional cases of which one doesn't speak. These things put into motion certain small entities which are usually the result of the decomposition of human beings and yet have a sufficient contact with the material world to be able to act there. But anyhow, if the action is of a lower order, the power is of a lower order, and it is something almost repugnant for one who is truly in relation with the higher forces.

To act in order to accomplish a work with the spontaneous powers of spiritual realisation, that is well understood. But one may say that everybody does that, because just the fact of thinking means that you are acting invisibly; and according to the power of your thought your action is more or less wide-spread. But to use small magical formulas to obtain a result is something that has no true relation with the spiritual life. From the spiritual point of view it appears even surprising that these things can always prove effective, because for each case the need is different; and how putting together certain words and making certain signs can always have an effect seems surprising.

When one wants to act spiritually and for some reason or other it is necessary, for example, to formulate words, the words come spontaneously and are exactly the words needed for the particular occasion. But things written beforehand which one repeats mechanically most of the time, without even knowing what one is saying and why one is saying it – it is difficult to see how this can always work. There is bound to be a great imprecision in the action. And one thing is certain, that this same formula cannot have exactly the same effect, and that one factor is indispensable for it to take effect: fear. The first thing is a kind of fear, a fright created in the person against whom the magic is done; for if he has no fear I am quite sure that it cannot have any effect or has so ridiculously small an effect that it's not worth speaking about it.

What opens the door to the action of these forces is fear, a kind of apprehension, the feeling that something is going to happen; and it is these vibrations of fear which put out certain forces from you, forces which give these entities the power to act.

THE MOTHER

Mother, can physical science by its progress open to occultism?

It does not call it "occultism", that's all. It is only a question of words.... They are making sensational discoveries which people with occult knowledge alredy knew thousands of years ago! They have made a long circuit and come to the same thing.

With the most recent discoveries in medicine, in the applied sciences, for instance, they are contacting in this way, with a wonder-struck interest, things which were known to certain sages a very, very long time ago. And then they present all this before you as new marvels – but indeed they are rather old, their marvels!

They will end up by practising occultism without knowing that they are doing so! For, in fact, as soon as one draws close, however slightly, to the truth of things and when one is sincere in one's search, not satisfied by mere appearances, when one really wants to find something and goes deep, penetrates behind appearances, then one begins to advance towards the truth of things; and as one comes closer to it, well, one finds again the same knowledge that others who began by going within have brought back from their inner discoveries.

Only the method and the path are different but the thing discovered will be the same, because there are not two things to be found, there is only one. It will necessarily be the same. It all depends on the path one follows; some go fast, others slowly, some go straight, others, as I said, go a long way round – and what labour! How they have laboured!... Besides, it is very respectable.

(*Silence*)

Now they are finding out that they can replace anaesthetics by hypnotism with infinitely better results. Well, hypnotism is a form – a form modernised in its expression – of occultism; a very limited, very small form of a very tiny power compared with occult power, but still it is a form of occultism which has been put in modern terms to make the thing modern. And I don't know if you have heard about these things, but they are very interesting from a certain point of view: for instance, this process of hypnotism has been tried on someone who had to have a skin-graft on a wound. I don't remember all the details now, but the arm had to remain attached to the leg for a fortnight.... If the person were immobilised by plaster and bandages and all sorts of things, at the end of the fortnight he wouldn't be able to move – everything would become stiff and he would need weeks of treatment to recover the free use of his arm. In this case, nothing was tied up, nothing was physically immobilised – no plaster, no bandages, nothing – the person was just hypnotised and told to keep his arm in that position. He kept it for a fortnight, without any effort, any difficulty, without any intervention from his will: it was the will of the hypnotiser which intervened. It was perfectly successful, the arm remained in the required position, and when the fortnight was over and the hypnotism removed, and the person was told, "Now you may move", he began to move! Well, that's a step forward.

They are soon going to meet – it will be nothing more than a question of words – then, if they are not too rigid, they can agree on the value given to the words!

THE MOTHER

Occult Worlds and Entities

... last week... I spoke of the "threshold of occultism". So a question is put to me about this occult world, that is to say, the world invisible to ordinary physical eyes, and I am asked for explanations or comments on the beings who live in these worlds which are invisible to ordinary eyes.

I am even told that I speak very often of negative entities, that is to say, of hostile formations, of small beings formed from the disintegration of human beings after their death – the disintegration of the vital or mental being at death – but that I have never spoken of the great beings, the magnificent beings or positive entities which help the evolution. I believe I have spoken to you about these quite often, but still I have been asked once again for explanations.

Well, the occult world is not one single region where everything is mixed, which only becomes occult because we can't see it. The occult world is a gradation of regions, one could perhaps say, of more and more etherial or subtle regions, anyway, those farther and farther removed in their nature from the physical materiality we ordinarily see. And each one of these domains is a world in itself, having its forms and inhabited by beings with a density, one might say, analogous to that of the domain in which they live. Just as in the physical world we are of the same materiality as the physical world, so in the vital world, in the mental world, in the overmind world and in the supramental world – and in many others, infinite others – there are beings which have a form whose substance is similar to the one of that world. This means that if you are able to enter consciously into that world with the part of your being which corresponds to that domain, you can move there quite objectively, as in the material world.

And there, there are as many, and even many more things to see and observe than in our poor little material world, which belongs to only *one* zone of this infinite gradation. You meet all sorts of things in these domains, and you need to make a study as profound, perhaps still more profound than in the physical world, to be able to know what is happening there, to have relations with the beings who live there.

It is obvious that as one goes farther, as it were, from the material world, the forms and consciousness of those beings are of a purity, beauty and perfection much higher than our ordinary physical forms. It is only in the nearest vital world, the one which is, so to say, mixed with our material life – though it lies beyond it and there is a zone where the vital is no longer mixed with the material world – of that material vital one can say that in some of its aspects it is even uglier than things here, for it is filled with a bad will which is not counterbalanced by the presence of the psychic being which, in the physical world, amends, corrects, puts right, directs this bad will. But it is rather a limited zone and, as soon as one goes beyond it, one can find and meet things that are not favourable to human life, beings not on the same scale as human existence, but having their own beauty and grandeur, with whom one may establish relations which may become quite pleasant and even useful.

Only, as I have already told you, it is not very prudent to venture into these domains without a previous initiation and, above all, a purification of nature which prevents you from entering there all weighed down and deformed by your desires, your passions, egoisms, fears and weaknesses. Before undertaking these activities one needs a complete preparation of self-purification and widening of the consciousness which is absolutely indispensable.

In these invisible worlds there are also regions which are the result of human mental formations. One can find there all one wants. In fact, one very often finds there exactly what one expects to find. There are hells, there are paradises, there are purgatories. There are all sorts of things in accordance with the different religions and their conceptions. These things have only a very relative existence, but with a relativity similar to that of material things here; that is to say, for someone who finds himself there, they are entirely real and their effects quite tangible. One needs an inner liberation, a wideness of the consciousness and a contact with a deeper and higher truth to be able to escape from the illusion of their reality. But this is something almost similar to what happens here: human beings here are mostly convinced that the only reality is the physical reality – the reality of what one can touch, can see – and for them, all that cannot be seen, cannot be touched, cannot be felt, is after all, proble-matical; well, what happens there is an identical pheno-menon. People who at the moment of death are con-vinced, for one reason or another, that they are going to paradise or maybe to hell, *do find* themselves there after their death; and for them it is truly a paradise or a hell. And it is extremely difficult to make them come out of it and go to a place which is more true, more real.

So it is difficult to speak of all these worlds, these innumerable worlds, in a few minutes. It is a knowledge which needs a lived experience of many years, thoroughly systematic, and which requires, as I said, an inner prepa-ration absolutely indispensable, to make it harmless.

We all get the chance to have a little contact – very partial, very superficial – with these worlds in our dreams. And the study of dreams itself already demands much time and care, and in itself may constitute a preparation for a deeper study of the invisible worlds.

THE MOTHER

Are there not accidents which are almost inevitable? I just read of a case cited by an American who had the gift of clairvoyance. A child was playing on a railway track, it was in danger. Suddenly the witness saw an apparition beside the child and he breathed a sigh of relief, thinking, "The child will be saved." But to his

> *great astonishment the apparition put its hand over*
> *the eyes of the child and threw it in some way under*
> *the train. This man was much troubled, he could not*
> *understand why a being whom he had taken for a*
> *higher being would push a child to its death.*

Certainly this may be true, but without having the vision oneself, one can't explain it.

It may be a question of two absolutely different things. Perhaps, indeed, it was its destiny, in the sense that it was the end of the life necessary for its psychic being, it was a death which had been predestined for some reason, because that can happen. Or perhaps it could be an adverse force which he took to be an angel of light, for generally people make this mistake – when they see an apparition they always think it is something heavenly. It is heavenly if you like, but it depends on what heaven it comes from!

It is a strange thing because.... Yes, the moment of unconsciousness, the slackening of consciousness may be translated by this someone putting the hand over the eyes.

One of the most common activities of these intolerable little entities which are in the human physical atmosphere and amuse themselves at men's expense, is to blind you to such an extent that when you look for something, and the thing is staring you in the face, you do not see it! This happens very often. You search in vain, you turn every-thing over, you look into all possible corners, but you don't find the thing. Then you give up the problem and some time later (precisely when "the hand over the eyes" is removed), you come back to the same place and it is exactly there where you have looked, quietly lying there, it had not stirred! Only you were unconscious, you did not see. This is a very, very frequent amusement of these little entities. They also take pleasure in removing things, then they put them back, but at times they also don't put them back! They displace them, indeed they have all sorts of little diversions. They are intolerable. Madame Blavatsky made much use of them, but I don't know how she managed to make them so amiable, because generally they are quite unpleasant.

I had the experience – among innumerable instances – but precisely of two very striking cases, of two opposite things, only it was not the same beings.... There are little beings like fairies who are very sweet, very obliging, but they are not always there, they come from time to time when it pleases them. I remember the time I used to cook for Sri Aurobindo; I was also doing many other things at the same time, so I often happened to leave the milk on the fire and go for some other work or to see something with him, to discuss with somebody, and truly I was not always aware of the time, I used to forget the milk on the fire. And whenever I forgot the milk on the fire, I felt suddenly (in those days I used to wear a sari) a little hand catching a fold of my sari and pulling it, like this. Then I used to run quickly and would see that the milk was just on the point of boiling over. This did not happen just once, but several times, and very clearly, like a little child's hand clutching and pulling.

The other story is of the days Sri Aurobindo had the habit of walking up and down in his rooms. He used to walk for several hours like that, it was his way of meditating. Only, he wanted to know the time, so a clock had been put in each room to enable him to see the time at any moment. There were three such clocks. One was in the room where I worked; it was, so to say, his starting-point. One day he came and asked, "What time is it?" He looked and the clock had stopped. He went into the next room, saying, "I shall see the time there" – the clock had stopped. And it had stopped at the same minute as the other, you understand, with the difference of a few seconds. He went to the third room... the clock had stopped. He continued walking three times like that – all the clocks had stopped! Then he returned to my room and said, "But this is impossible! This is a bad joke!" and all the clocks, one after the other, started working again. I saw it myself, you know, it was a charming incident. He was angry, he said, "This is a bad joke!" And all the clocks started going again!

THE MOTHER

Have these vital beings a psychic being?

No, I said that the first thing they have to do to incarnate is to drive away the psychic being of the person whom they possess. That may happen from the very birth. There are children who are almost still-born; they are taken to be dead and suddenly they revive – this means that a vital being has incarnated in them. I have known such cases. This may happen also in the course of an illness: someone is very ill and gradually he lets go the contact with the psychic being, then, in a swoon or some other similar state, he cuts the contact entirely and the vital being rushes into the body. I have known cases of this kind also. Or it may be a slow action: the vital being enters into the atmosphere of the person, goes on influencing him and finally brings about illness, attacks, specially mental illness; then a time comes when the connection with the psychic being is entirely cut and the vital being takes possession of the body. There are cases of people falling very ill and coming out of the illness altogether different from what they were. Very often it is this that happens.

You have said that these beings of the vital world are attracted by the spiritual life. Why?

They are attracted, but this does not mean that they have decided sincerely to follow the spiritual life. The chief characteristic of these beings is falsehood: their nature is made of deceit. They have a power for illusion; they can take the appearance of divine beings or higher beings, they can appear in a dazzling light, but truly sincere people are not deceived, they immediately feel something that warns them. But if one likes the marvellous, the unexpected, if one loves fantastic things, if one likes to live a romance, one is likely to be easily deceived.

Not long ago there was a historical instance, that of Hitler, who was in contact with a being whom he considered to be the Supreme: this being came and gave him advice, told him all that he had to do. Hitler used to retire into solitude and remain there as long as it was necessary to come into contact with his "guide" and receive from him inspirations which he carried out later very faithfully. This being which Hitler took for the Supreme was quite plainly an Asura, one who is called the "Lord of Falsehood" in occultism, but who proclaimed himself the "Lord of the Nations". He had a shining appearance, he could mislead anybody except one who really had occult knowledge and could see what was there behind the appearance. He would have deceived anybody, he was truly splendid. Generally he used to appear to Hitler wearing a silver cuirass and helmet; a kind of flame came out of his head and there was an atmosphere of dazzling light around him, so dazzling that Hitler could hardly look at him. He used to tell Hitler everything that had to be done – he played with him as with a monkey or a mouse. He had decided clearly to make Hitler commit all possible extravagances till the day he would break his neck, which did happen. But cases like this are frequent, though on a smaller scale, of course.

Hitler was a very good medium, he had great mediumistic capacities, but he lacked intelligence and discrimination. This being could tell him anything whatever and he swallowed it all. It was he who pushed Hitler little by little. And he was doing this as a distraction, he did not take life seriously. For these beings men are very tiny things with whom they play, as a cat plays with a mouse, till finally they eat them up.

Are mentally deranged people possessed?

Yes, unless there is a physical lesion, a defect in the formation or an accident, a congestion. In all other cases it is always a possession. The proof of it is that if a person is brought to you who is altogether mentally deranged, if he has a lesion, he cannot be cured, while if there is no physical lesion, if it is a possession, then one can cure him. Unfortunately these things happen only to people who like them; there must be in the being much ambition, vanity, combined with much stupidity and a terrible pride – it is on such things that those beings play. I have known cases like that, of persons who were partially possessed, and I succeeded in freeing them from the beings who possessed them. Naturally they felt some relief, a kind of ease for a time, but it did not last long; almost immediately it wore off and they thought: "Now I have become quite an ordinary creature, whereas before I was an exceptional being!" They used to feel within them an exceptional power, even if it was a power to do evil, and they were satisfied with it. So what did they do? They called back with all their force the power they had lost! Of course, the being that had been destroyed could not come back, but as these beings exist in thousands it was replaced by another. I have seen this happen three times consecutively in a case, so much so that in the end I had to tell the person: "I am tired, get rid of it yourself, I am no longer interested!"

THE MOTHER

In all religious monuments, in monuments considered the most... well, as belonging to the highest religion, whether in France or any other country or Japan – it was never the same temples or churches nor the same gods, and yet my experience was everywhere almost the same, with very small differences – I saw that whatever concentrated force there was in the church depended exclusively upon the faithful, the faith of the devotees. And there was still a difference between the force as it really was and the force as they felt it. For instance, I saw in one of the most beautiful cathedrals of France, which, from the artistic point of view, is one of the most magnificent monuments imaginable – in the most sacred spot I saw an *enormous* black, vital spider which had made its web and spread it over the whole place, and was catching in it and then absorbing all the forces emanating from people's devotion, their prayers and all that. It was not a very cheering sight; the people who were there and were praying, felt a divine touch, they received all kinds of boons from their prayers, and yet what was there was this, this thing. But they had their faith which could change that evil thing into something good in them; they had their faith. So, truly, if *I* had gone and told them "Do you think you are praying to God? It is an enormous vital spider that's feeding upon all your forces!", that would really not have been very charitable. And that's how it is most of the time, almost everywhere; it is a vital force which is there, for these vital entities feed upon the vibration of human emotions, and very few people, very few, an insignificant number, go to church or temple with a true religious feeling, that is, not to pray and beg for something from God but to offer themselves, give thanks, aspire, give themselves. There is hardly one in a million who does that. So they do not have the power of changing the atmosphere. Perhaps when they are there, they manage to get across, break through and go somewhere and touch something divine. But the large majority of people who go only because of superstition, egoism and self-interest, create an atmosphere of this kind, and that is what you breathe in when you go to a church or temple. Only, as you go there with a very good feeling, you tell yourself, "Oh, what a quiet place for meditation!"

I am sorry, but that's how it is. I tell you I have

deliberately tried this experiment a little everywhere. Maybe I found some very tiny places, like a tiny village church at times, where there was a very quiet little spot for meditation, very still, very silent, where there was some aspiration; but this was so rare! I have seen the beautiful churches of Italy, magnificent places; they were full of these vital beings and full of terror. I remember painting in a basilica of Venice, and while I was working, in the confessional a priest was hearing the confession of a poor woman. Well, it was truly a frightful sight! I don't know what the priest was like, what his character was, he could not be seen – you know, don't you? that they are not seen, they are shut up in a box and receive the confession through a grille. There was such a dark and sucking power over him, and that poor woman was in such a state of fearful terror that it was truly painful to see it. And all these people believe this is something holy! But it is a web of the hostile vital forces which use all this to feed upon. Besides, in the invisible world hardly any beings love to be worshipped, except those of the vital. These, as I said, are quite pleased by it. And then, it gives them importance. They are puffed up with pride and feel very happy, and when they can get a herd of people to worship them they are quite satisfied....

For example, there are so many of these entities called Kali – who are given, besides, quite terrible appearances – so many are even placed in houses as the family-goddess; they are full of a terrible vital force! I knew people who were so frightened of the Kali they had at home that indeed they trembled to make the least mistake, for when catastrophes came they thought it was Kali who sent them! It is a frightful thing, thought. I know them, those entities. I know them very well, but they are vital beings, vital forms which, so to say, are given a form by human thought, and what forms! And to think that men worship such terrible and monstrous things....

From this point of view, it is good that for some time men get out of this religious atmosphere, so full of fear, and this sort of blind, superstitious submission of which the hostile forces have taken a dreadful advantage. The period of denial, positivism, is from this viewpoint quite indispensable in order to free men from superstition. It is only when one comes out of that and the abject submission to monstrous vital forces that one can rise to truly spiritual heights and there become the collaborator and true instrument of the forces of Truth, the real Consciousness, the true Power.

One must leave all this far behind before one can climb higher.

THE MOTHER

There are some human beings who are like vampires. What are they and why are they like that?

They are not human; there is only a human form or appearance. They are incarnations of beings from the world that is just next to the physical, beings who live on the plane which we call the vital world. It is a world of all the desires and impulses and passions and of movements of violence and greed and cunning and every kind of ignorance; but all the dynamisms too are there, all the life-energies and all the powers. The beings of this world have by their nature a strange grip over the material world and can exercise upon it a sinister influence. Some of them are formed out of the remains of the human being that persist after death in the vital atmosphere near to the earth-plane. His desires and hungers still float there and remain in form even after the dissolution of the body; often they are moved to go on manifesting and satisfying themselves and the birth of these creatures of the vital world is the consequence. But these are minor beings and, if they can be very troublesome, it is yet not impossible to deal with them. There are others, far more dangerous, who have never been in human form; never were they born into a human body upon earth, for most often they refuse to accept this way of birth because it is slavery to matter and they prefer to remain in their own world, powerful and mischievous, and to control earthly beings from there. For, if they do not want to be born on earth, they do want to be in contact with the physical nature, but without being bound by it. Their method is to try first to cast their influence upon a man; then they enter slowly into his atmosphere and in the end may get complete possession of him, driving out entirely the real human soul and personality. These creatures, when in possession of an earthly body, may have the human appearance but they have not a human nature. Their habit is to draw upon the life-force of human beings; they attack and capture vital power wherever they can and feed upon it. If they come into your atmosphere, you suddenly feel depressed and exhausted; if you are near them for some time you fall sick; if you live with one of them, it may kill you.

But how is one to get such creatures out of one's environment when they are once there?

The vital power incarnated in these beings is of a very material kind and it is effective only within a short distance. Ordinarily, if you do not live in the same house or if you are not in the same company with them, you do not come within their influence. But if you open some channel of connection or communication, through letters, for example, then you make possible an interchange of forces and are liable to be influenced by them even from a far distance. The wisest way with these beings is to cut off all connection and have nothing to do with them – unless indeed you have great occult knowledge and power and have learned how to cover and protect yourself – but even then it is always a dangerous thing to move about with them. To hope to transform them, as some people do, is a vain illusion; for they do not want to be transformed. They have no intention of allowing any transformation and all effort in that direction is useless.

These beings, when in the human body, are not often conscious of what they really are. Sometimes they have a vague feeling that they are not quite human in the ordinary way. But still there are cases where they are conscious and very conscious; not only do they know that they do not belong to humanity but they know what they are, act in that knowledge and deliberately pursue their ends. The beings of the vital world are powerful by their very nature; when to their power they add knowledge, they become doubly dangerous. There is nothing to be done with these creatures; you should avoid having any dealings with them unless you have the power to crush and destroy them. If you are forced into contact with them, beware of the spell they can cast. These vital beings, when they manifest on the physical plane, have always a great hypnotic power; for the centre of their consciousness is in the vital world and not in the material and they are not veiled and dwarfed by the material consciousness as human beings are.

THE MOTHER

Magic, Miracles and the Planchette

In occultism there is the "rebound". You send out a bad thought, it returns to you as an attack. That is exactly one of the reasons why you must have a complete control over your feelings, sensations, thoughts, for if you become angry with someone or think badly of him, or if, still worse, you wish him ill, well, in your very dream you see this person coming with an extreme violence to attack you. Then, if you do not know these things, you say, "Why, I was right in having bad thoughts against him!" But in fact, it is not at all that. It is your own thought that comes back to you. And the person may be absolutely unaware of all that has happened, for – and this is one of the commonest laws in occultism – if you make a formatioh, for instance a mental formation that an accident or something unpleasant should happen to a certain person and you send out this formation, if it so happens that this person is in a very high state of consciousness, does not at all wish anything bad, is quite indifferent and disinterested in the affair, the formation will come up against his atmosphere and instead of entering will rebound upon the one who has made it. In this way serious accidents have taken place. There were certain people who practised that low deformation of occultism which is called magic and

they had made formations through magic against someone. But this person happened to be far above this and
could not be touched by those formations. So they
returned upon those people, fatally. If they had made a
formation of death, it would have been they who died.

THE MOTHER

*"They [powers] have to be used in the same way as
they came. They come by union with the Divine.
They must be used by the will of the Divine and not
for display."*

Questions and Answers 1929 (14 April)

If you use power to show that you possess it, it becomes so
full of falsehood and untruth that finally it disappears. But
it is not always thus, because as I said at the beginning,
when it concerns a power like the power of healing or the
power of changing an altogether external thing – of
making an unfavourable circumstance favourable, of
finding lost objects, all these countless little "miracles"
which are found in all religions – it is much more easy and
even more effective to do these "miracles" with the help
of the entities of the vital world which are not always
recommendable, far from it; and then these beings make
fun of you. This begins very well, very brilliantly, and
usually finishes very badly.

I know the story of a man who had a few small powers
and indulged in all kinds of so-called "spiritualist" practices, and through repeated exercises he had succeeded in
coming into conscious contact with what he called a
"spirit". This man was doing business; he was a financier

and was even a speculator. His relations with his "spirit" were of a very practical kind! This spirit used to tell him when the stocks and shares would go up and when they would come down; it told him, "Sell this", "Buy that" – it gave him very precise financial particulars. For years he had been listening to his "spirit" and had followed it, and was fantastically successful; he became tremendously rich and naturally boasted a lot about the spirit which "guided" him. He used to tell everybody, "You see, it is really worthwhile learning how to put oneself in contact with these spirits." But one day he met a man who was a little wiser, who told him, "Take care." He did not listen to him, he was swollen with his power and ambition. And it was then that his "spirit" gave him a last advice, "Now you can become the richest man in the world. Your ambition will be fulfilled. You have only to follow my direction. Do this: put all that you have into this transaction and you will become the richest man in the world." The stupid fool did not even realise the trap laid for him: for years he had followed his "guide" and succeeded, so he followed the last direction; and he lost everything, to the last penny.

So you see, these are small entities who make fun of you, and to make sure of you they work these little miracles to encourage you, and when they feel that you are well trapped, they play a fine trick upon you and it is all over with you.

THE MOTHER

"Ambition has been the undoing of many Yogis....
"A story is told of a Yogi who had attained

wonderful powers. He was invited by his disciples to a great dinner. It was served on a big low table. The disciples asked their Master to show his power in some way. He knew he should not, but the seed of ambition was there in him and he thought, 'After all, it is a very innocent thing and it may prove to them that such things are possible and teach them the greatness of God.' So he said, 'Take away the table, but only the table, let the table-cloth remain as it is with all the dishes upon it.' The disciples cried out, 'Oh, that cannot be done, everything will fall down.' But he insisted and they removed the table from under the cloth. Lo, the miracle! The cloth and all that was upon it remained there just as though the table was underneath. The disciples wondered. But all on a sudden the Master jumped up and rushed out screaming and crying, 'Nevermore shall I have a disciple, nevermore! Woe is me! I have betrayed my God.'"

Questions and Answers 1929 (14 April)

This is a temptation that every teacher meets at each step, for the very simple reason that ordinary humanity, in a general way, not being in personal contact with the divine powers, understands nothing of what an illumined consciousness may be and asks for material proofs. It is on this demand that most religions are established and, for reasons which I may very frankly call "political", they have put at the origin of their religion a more or less considerable number of miracles as having been performed by the founders, and they have thus more or less crudely encouraged among ignorant people the taste, the necessity for seeing what they call "miracles" in order to believe in the divine power of a person. This is an extraordinary ignorance, because it is not at all necessary to have a divine power or consciousness to perform miracles. It is infinitely more easy to perform miracles with the help of small entities of the vital world who are material enough to be in touch with the physical world and act upon it than to live in the consciousness of the higher regions and to work upon Nature only through the intermediary of all the other domains. It has been repeated over and over again to all human intellects that the proof of a being's divinity is that he can raise the dead, cure maladies, and do many other things of the same kind (except making a fool wise).* Well, I guarantee that this is not a proof; it proves only one thing, that these "Masters" are in contact with the powers of the vital world and that with the help of those beings they can perform these miracles, that's all.

THE MOTHER

What kind of forces can be called up by using the planchette, and how is it done?

Oh! Oh!... Do you mean automatic writing?

Yes, Mother.

That depends on the people who do it. Sometimes there

---

* Mother added later: This is a Mohammedan story, I believe. As it was said that Jesus raised the dead, healed the sick, made the dumb speak, gave sight to the blind, one day an idiot was brought to him, to be made intelligent and Jesus ran away! "Why did you run away?" he was asked. "I can do everything," he answered, "except give intelligence to an idiot."

are no forces at all! It is the mental and vital vibrations of the people who use the planchette, and it is their own subconscious ideas which they bring up, ninety-eight times out of a hundred.* If they are in contact with invisible entities, it may be all sorts of things but nothing very advisable!

Almost with certainty it could be said that it is not what people think it is, in the sense that most often they try to evoke what they call the "spirit" of a dead person, a relative or a friend or someone they loved and with whom they wish to remain in touch; and besides, they ask them the most foolish questions. Fortunately they don't succeed in disturbing them....

From this point of view one can say that if you had a relation of deep and sincere love with someone who has passed away, left his body, and if you are calm and strong enough yourself, this person may choose to take shelter vitally in your atmosphere – the atmosphere of the one he loves – for a more or less long period. In this case it means that the relation was very close, very intimate, and if you are not altogether materialistic to the point of not having any direct mental perception, you can remain in mental contact with this person, in communication with him. It is a rather exceptional case, for usually if your atmosphere is calm and strong enough to be able to truly serve as a protection, the person who has left his body enters into a deep rest there, and it is not at all good to disturb it; and the best thing you can do is to enfold this person with your love and leave him in peace.

---

* Later Mother added the following remark: "I say ninety times out of a hundred, for there are exceptions – I know of some – but they are so rare that it is better not to speak about them."

Therefore, even if it were possible to enter into communication with him by this means, which I would call very crude, it would be improper to do so. But usually, people who have the capacity, the faculties required to serve as a shelter for some time, a transitional shelter for those who have gone, do not have this ridiculous idea of disturbing the rest of the one they love by tapping on a planchette... fortunately!

But those who indulge in this exercise, an exercise of unhealthy curiosity, get what they deserve; for the atmosphere we live in is filled with a great number of small vital entities which are born of unsatisfied desires, vital movements of a very low type, also the decomposition of larger beings of the vital world; indeed, it is swarming with them, you see. It is surely a protection that most people do not see what is going on in this vital atmosphere, for it is not especially pleasant; but if they have the presumption to want to come into contact with it and set about trying automatic writing or table-turning or... indeed, anything of this kind, out of an unhealthy curiosity, well, what happens is that one of these small entities or several of them have fun at their expense and collect all the necessary indications from their subconscious mind and then furnish these things to them as clear proofs that they are the person who has been called!

I could write a book for you with all the examples I have known of these stories, for people are very proud of doing things like this and immediately write them down, giving "proofs" of the truth of the experience which are so ridiculous that they should be enough to show them that someone was making fun of them! I had another instance, very recently, of somebody who fancied that he had entered into contact with Sri Aurobindo and was receiving sensational revelations from him – that was comical in the extreme.

But anyway, as a rule, it is – oh! most often – it is your own forces, your subconscious mental and vital forces which you put into the planchette – and you make sensational revelations to yourself! One can do many things in this way.... Once I wanted to prove to people that what they were evoking was nothing but themselves; so I had a little fun, simply with a concentration of the will, tapping the furniture, making tables walk and, well!... As for automatic writing, you only have to withdraw your conscious will into yourself, to let your hand go – just like this (*gesture*) – and leave it free, and then the hand will begin to make movements; but there is a little part in you which is interested and would like these movements to make sense and this little part appeals to the subconscious mind which begins to make sensational revelations. Inded, it is a booby-trap, all this business, unless one does it scientifically – but then, scientifically, one realises that it leads to nothing, nothing at all except just passing your time in what you consider an interesting way.

In some cases vital entities really get hold of you, and there it is dangerous. But fortunately these cases are not very frequent. Then it becomes very dangerous.

A very long time ago when I was in France, I knew the case of a man who, through practices of this kind, had put himself into contact with a vital entity. This man happened to be a gambler and he spent his time speculating and playing roulette. He spent part of the year at Monte Carlo playing roulette and the rest of the time he lived in the south of France and speculated on the Stock Exchange. And now, some being was really using him – it was through automatic writing – using him, and for years it gave him absolutely precise, exact indications. When he played roulette it used to tell him, "Bid on this number or this place", and he would win. Naturally he just worshipped this "spirit" which gave him such sensational revelations. And at the Exchange it also told him, "Speculate on this or on that" and gave him all the indications. This man became colossally rich. He used to boast to all his friends about the method by which he had grown rich.

Someone put him on his guard, told him, "Be careful, this doesn't look very honest, you should not trust this spirit." He fell out with this person. A few days later he was in Monte Carlo and... He always played for high stakes, you see; since, naturally, he always won and would break the bank, he was much feared. Then the spirit told him, "Stake everything, *everything* you have on this...." He did, and at a single stroke lost everything! And yet, he still had some money left from his Stock Exchange speculations. He said to himself, "It is bad luck." Again he received a very precise indication, "Do this", as usual. And he did it – he was completely cleaned out! And to finish the job, the spirit told him, just for the fun of it, "Now, you are going to commit suicide. Put a bullet through your head". And he was so much under its influence, he did so.... That's the end of the story. And this is an authentic story. So, the least one can say is that it is dangerous, it is much better not to indulge in occupations of this kind.

No! Either they are rather senseless amusements or else they are unwholesome occupations.

THE MOTHER

VI

HIDDEN WORLDS AND EVOLUTIONARY FORCES

Our earth is a fragment and a residue;
Her power is packed with the stuff of greater worlds
And steeped in their colour-lustres dimmed by her drowse;
An atavism of higher births is hers,
Her sleep is stirred by their buried memories
Recalling the lost spheres from which they fell.
Unsatisfied forces in her bosom move;
They are partners of her greater growing fate
And her return to immortality;

SRI AUROBINDO
Savitri, Book Two, Canto One

A difficult evolution from below
Called a masked intervention from above;
Else this great, blind inconscient universe
Could never have disclosed its hidden mind,
Or even in blinkers worked in beast and man
The Intelligence that devised the cosmic scheme.

SRI AUROBINDO
Savitri, Book Two, Canto Four

HIDDEN WORLDS AND EVOLUTIONARY FORCES

Existence and Influence of Hidden Worlds

It is a fact that mankind almost from the beginning of its existence or so far back as history or tradition can go, has believed in the existence of other worlds and in the possibility of communication between their powers and beings and the human race....

It is evident that the beliefs of the past are not a sufficient basis for knowledge, even though they cannot be entirely neglected: for a belief is a mental construction and may be a wrong building; it may often answer to some inner intimation and then it has a value, but, as often as not, it disfigures the intimation, usually by a translation into terms familiar to our physical and objective experience, such as that which converted the hierarchy of the planes into a physical hierarchy or geographical space-extension, turned the rarer heights of subtle substance into material heights and placed the abodes of the gods on the summits of physical mountains. All truth supraphysical or physical must be founded not on mental belief alone, but on experience, – but in each case experience must be of the kind, physical, subliminal or spiritual, which is appropriate to the order of the truths into which we are empowered to enter; their validity and significance must be scrutinised, but according to their own law and by a consciousness which can enter into them and not according to the law of another domain or by a consciousness which is capable only of truths of another order; so alone can we be sure of our steps and enlarge firmly our sphere of knowledge.

If we scrutinise the intimations of supraphysical world-realities which we receive in our inner experience and compare with it the account of such intimations that has continued to come down to us from the beginnings of human knowledge, and if we attempt an interpretation and a summarised order, we shall find that what this inner experience most intimately conveys to us is the existence and action upon us of larger planes of being and consciousness than the purely material plane, with its restricted existence and action, of which we are aware in our narrow terrestrial formula. These domains of larger being are not altogether remote and separate from our own being and consciousness; for, though they subsist in themselves and have their own play and process and formulations of existence and experience, yet at the same time they penetrate and envelop the physical plane with their invisible presence and influences, and their powers seem to be here in the material world itself behind its action and objects. There are two main orders of experience in our contact with them; one is purely subjective, though in its subjectivity sufficiently vivid and palpable, the other is more objective. In the subjective order, we find that what shapes itself to us as a life-intention, life-impulse, life-formulation here, already exists in a larger, more subtle, more plastic range of possibilities, and these pre-existent forces and formations are pressing upon us to realise themselves in the physical world also; but only a part succeeds in getting through and even that emerges partially in a form and circumstance more proper to the system of terrestrial law and sequence. This precipitation takes place, normally, without our knowledge; we are not aware of the action of these powers, forces and influences upon us, but take them as formations of our own life and mind, even when our reason or will repudiates them and strives not to be mastered: but when we go inwards away from the restricted surface consciousness and develop a subtler sense and deeper awareness, we begin to get an intimation of the origin of these movements and are able to watch their action and process, to accept or reject or modify, to allow them passage and use of our mind and will and our life and members or refuse it. In the same way we become aware of larger domains of mind, a play, experience, formation of a greater plasticity, a teeming profusion of all possible mental formulations, and we feel their contacts with us and their powers and influences acting upon our parts of mind in the same occult manner as those others that act upon our parts of life. This kind of experience is, primarily, of a purely subjective character, a pressure of ideas, suggestions, emotional formations, impulsions to sensation, action, dynamic experience. However large a part of this pressure may be traced to our own subliminal self or to the siege of universal Mind-forces or Life-forces belonging to our own world, there is an element which bears the stamp of another origin, an insistent supraterrestrial character.

But the contacts do not stop here: for there is also an opening of our mind and life parts to a great range of subjective-objective experiences in which these planes present themselves no longer as extensions of subjective being and consciousness, but as worlds; for the experiences there are organised as they are in our own world, but on a different plan, with a different process and law of action and in a substance which belongs to a supraphysical Nature. This organisation includes, as on our earth, the existence of beings who have or take forms, manifest themselves or are naturally manifested in an embodying substance, but a substance other than ours, a subtle substance tangible only to subtle sense, a supraphysical form-matter. These worlds and beings may have nothing to do with ourselves and our life, they may exercise no action upon us; but often also they enter into secret communication with earth-existence, obey or embody and are the intermediaries and instruments of the cosmic powers and influences of which we have a subjective experience, or themselves act by their own initiation upon the terrestrial world's life and motives and happenings. It is possible to receive help or guidance or harm or misguidance from these beings; it is possible even to become subject to their influence, to be possessed by their invasion or domination, to be instrumentalised by them for their good or evil purpose. At times the progress of earthly life seems to be a vast field of battle between supraphysical Forces of either character, those that strive to uplift, encourage and illumine and those that strive to deflect, depress or prevent or even shatter our upward evolution or the soul's self-expression in the material universe. Some of these Beings, Powers or Forces are such that we think of them as divine; they are luminous, benignant or powerfully helpful: there are others that are Titanic, gigantic or demoniac, inordinate Influences, instigators or creators often of vast and formidable inner upheavals or of actions that overpass the normal human measure. There may also be an awareness of influences, presences, beings that do not seem to belong to other worlds beyond us but are here as a hidden element behind the veil in terrestrial nature. As contact with the supraphysical is possible, a contact can also take place subjective or objective, – or at least objectivised, – between our own consciousness and the consciousness of other once embodied beings who have passed into a supraphysical status in these other regions of existence. It is possible also to pass beyond a subjective contact or a subtle-sense perception and, in certain subliminal states of consciousness, to enter actually into other worlds and know something of their secrets. It is the more objective order of other-worldly experience that seized most the imagination of mankind in the past, but it was put by popular belief into a gross-objective statement which unduly assimilated these phenomena to those of the physical world with which we are familiar; for it is the normal tendency of our mind to turn everything into forms or symbols proper to its own kind and terms of experience.

This has always been, put into its most generalised terms, the normal range and character of other-worldly belief and experience in all periods of the past of the race; names and forms differ, but the general features have been strikingly similar in all countries and ages. What exact value are we to put upon these persistent beliefs or upon this mass of supernormal experience? It is not possible for anyone who has had these contacts with any intimacy and not only by scattered abnormal accidents, to put them aside as mere superstition or hallucination; for they are too insistent, real, effective, organic in their pressure, too constantly confirmed by their action and results to be so flung aside: an appreciation, an interpretation, a mental organisation of this side of our capacity of experience is indispensable.

SRI AUROBINDO

Not only are there physical realities which are supra-sensible, but, if evidence and experience are at all a test of truth, there are also senses which are supraphysical* and can not only take cognisance of the realities of the material world without the aid of the corporeal sense-organs, but can bring us into contact with other realities, supraphysical and belonging to another world – included, that is to say, in an organisation of conscious experiences that are dependent on some other principle than the gross Matter of which our suns and earths seem to be made.

Constantly asserted by human experience and belief since the origins of thought, this truth, now that the necessity of an exclusive preoccupation with the secrets of the material world no longer exists, begins to be justified by new-born forms of scientific research. The increasing evidences, of which only the most obvious and outward are established under the name of telepathy with its cognate phenomena, cannot long be resisted except by minds shut up in the brilliant shell of the past, by intellects limited in spite of their acuteness through the limitation of their field of experience and inquiry, or by those who confuse enlightenment and reason with the faithful repe-tition of the formulas left to us from a bygone century and the jealous conservation of dead or dying intellectual dogmas.

It is true that the glimpse of supraphysical realities acquired by methodical research has been imperfect and is yet ill-affirmed; for the methods used are still crude and defective. But these rediscovered subtle senses have at least been found to be true witnesses to physical facts

---

* *Sūkṣma indriya*, subtle organs, existing in the subtle body (*sūkṣma deha*), and the means of subtle vision and experience (*sūkṣma dṛṣṭi*).

beyond the range of the corporeal organs. There is no justification, then, for scouting them as false witnesses when they testify to supraphysical facts beyond the domain of the material organisation of consciousness. Like all evidence, like the evidence of the physical senses themselves, their testimony has to be controlled, scrutinised and arranged by the reason, rightly translated and rightly related, and their field, laws and processes determined. But the truth of great ranges of experience whose objects exist in a more subtle substance and are perceived by more subtle instruments than those of gross physical Matter, claims in the end the same validity as the truth of the material universe. The worlds beyond exist: they have their universal rhythm, their grand lines and formations, their self-existent laws and mighty energies, their just and luminous means of knowledge. And here on our physical existence and in our physical body they exercise their influences; here also they organise their means of manifestation and commission their messengers and their witnesses.

SRI AUROBINDO

The physical is not the only world; there are others that we become aware of through dream records, through the subtle senses, through influences and contacts, through imagination, intuition and vision. There are worlds of a larger subtler life than ours, vital worlds; worlds in which Mind builds its own forms and figures, mental worlds; psychic worlds which are the soul's home; others above with which we have little contact. In each of us there is a mental plane of consciousness, a psychic, a vital, a subtle physical as well as the gross physical and material plane. The same planes are repeated in the consciousness of general Nature. It is when we enter or contact these other planes that we come into connection with the worlds above the physical. In sleep we leave the physical body, only a subconscient residue remaining, and enter all planes and all sorts of worlds. In each we see scenes, meet beings, share in happenings, come across formations, influences, suggestions which belong to these planes. Even when we are awake, part of us moves in these planes, but their activity goes on behind the veil; our waking minds are not aware of it. Dreams are often only incoherent constructions of our subconscient, but others are records (often much mixed and distorted) or transcripts of experiences in these supraphysical planes. When we do sadhana, this kind of dream becomes very common; then subconscious dreams cease to predominate.

The forces and beings of the vital world have a great influence on human beings. The vital world is on one side a world of beauty, – the poet, artist, musician are in close contact with it; it is also a world of powers and passions, lusts and desires, – our own lusts and desires, and passions and ambitions can put us into connection with the vital worlds and their forces and beings. It is again a world of things dark, dangerous and horrible. Nightmares like X's are contacts with this side of the vital plane. Its influences are also the source of much in men that is demoniac, dirty, cruel and base.

SRI AUROBINDO

... all our spiritual and psychic experience bears affirmative witness, brings us always a constant and, in its main principles, an invariable evidence of the existence of higher worlds, freer planes of existence. Not having bound ourselves down, like so much of modern thought, to the dogma that only physical experience or experience based upon the physical sense is true, the analysis of physical experience by the reason alone verifiable, and all else only result of physical experience and physical existence and anything beyond this an error, self-delusion and hallucination, we are free to accept this evidence and to admit the reality of these planes. We see that they are, practically, different harmonies from the harmony of the physical universe; they occupy, as the word "plane" suggests, a different level in the scale of being and adopt a different system and ordering of its principles. We need not inquire, for our present purpose, whether they coincide in time and space with our own world or move in a different field of space and in another stream of time, – in either case it is in a more subtle substance and with other movements. All that directly concerns us is to know whether they are different universes, each complete in itself and in no way meeting, intercrossing or affecting the others, or are rather different scales of one graded and interwoven system of being, parts therefore of one complex universal system. The fact that they can enter into the field of our mental consciousness would naturally suggest the validity of the second alternative, but it would not by itself be altogether conclusive. But what we find is that these higher planes are actually at every moment acting upon and in communication with our own plane of being, although this action is naturally not present to our ordinary waking or outer consciousness, because that is for the most part limited to a reception and utilisation of the contacts of the physical world: but the moment we either go back into our subliminal being or enlarge our waking consciousness beyond the scope of the physical contacts, we become aware of something of this higher action. We find even that the human being can project himself partially into these higher planes under certain conditions, even while in the body; *a fortiori* must he be able to do it when out of the body, and to do it then completely, since there is no longer the disabling condition of the physical life bound down to the body. The consequences of this relation and this power of transference are of immense importance. On the one side they immediately justify, at any rate as an actual possibility, the ancient tradition of at least a temporary sojourn of the human conscious being in other worlds than the physical after the dissolution of the physical body. On the other side they open to us the possibility of an action of the higher planes on the material existence which can liberate the powers they represent, the powers of life, mind and spirit for the evolutionary intention inherent within Nature by the very fact of their embodiment in Matter.

SRI AUROBINDO

Action of Higher Worlds and Evolution

... we find these higher worlds in our vision and experience of them to be in no way based upon the material universe, in no way its results, but rather greater terms of being, larger and freer ranges of consciousness, and all the action of the material plane looks more like the result and not the origin of these greater terms, derivatory from them, even partly dependent on them in its evolutionary endeavour. Immense ranges of powers, influences, phenomena descend covertly upon us from the Overmind and the higher mental and vital ranges, but of these only a part, a selection, as it were, or restricted number can stage and realise themselves in the order of the physical world; the rest await their time and proper circumstance for revelation in physical term and form, for their part in the terrestrial* evolution which is at the same time an evolution of all the powers of the Spirit.

This character of the other worlds defeats all our attempts to give the premier importance to our own plane of being and to our own part in the mundane manifestation. We do not create God as a myth of our consciousness, but are instruments for a progressive manifestation of the Divine in the material being. We do not create the gods, his powers, but rather such divinity as we manifest is the partial reflection and the shaping here of eternal godheads. We do not create the higher planes, but are intermediaries by which they reveal their light, power, beauty in whatever form and scope can be given to them by Nature-force on the material plane. It is the pressure of the Life-world which enables life to evolve and develop here in the forms we already know; it is that increasing pressure which drives it to aspire in us to a greater revelation of itself and will one day deliver the mortal from his subjection to the narrow limitations of his present

---

* Necessarily, by terrestrial we do not mean this one earth and its period of duration, but use earth in the wider root-sense of the Vedantic Prithivi, the earth-principle creating habitations of physical form for the soul.

incompetent and restricting physicality. It is the pressure of the Mind-world which evolves and develops mind here and helps us to find a leverage for our mental self-uplifting and expansion, so that we may hope to enlarge continually our self of intelligence and even to break the prison-walls of our matter-bound physical mentality. It is the pressure of the supramental and spiritual worlds which is preparing to develop here the manifest power of the Spirit and by it open our being on the physical plane into the freedom and infinity of the superconscient Divine; that contact, that pressure can alone liberate from the apparent Inconscience, which was our starting-point, the all-conscient Godhead concealed in us.

SRI AUROBINDO

Our material world is the result of all the others, for the other principles have all descended into Matter to create the physical universe, and every particle of what we call Matter contains all of them implicit in itself; their secret action... is involved in every moment of its existence and every movement of its activity. And as Matter is the last word of the descent, so it is also the first word of the ascent; as the powers of all these planes, worlds, grades, degrees are involved in the material existence, so are they all capable of evolution out of it. It is for this reason that material being does not begin and end with gases and chemical compounds and physical forces and movements, with nebulae and suns and earths, but evolves life, evolves mind, must evolve eventually Supermind and the higher degrees of the spiritual existence. Evolution comes by the unceasing pressure of the supra-material planes on the

material compelling it to deliver out of itself their principles and powers which might conceivably otherwise have
slept imprisoned in the rigidity of the material formula.
This would even so have been improbable, since their
presence there implies a purpose of deliverance; but still
this necessity from below is actually very much aided by a
kindred superior pressure.

SRI AUROBINDO

A secret continuous action of the higher powers and
principles from their own planes upon terrestrial being
and nature through the subliminal self, which is itself a
projection from those planes into the world born of the
Inconscience, must have an effect and a significance. Its
first effect has been the liberation of Life and Mind out of
Matter; its last effect has been to assist the emergence of a
spiritual consciousness, a spiritual will and spiritual sense
of existence in the terrestrial being so that he is no longer
solely preoccupied with his outermost life or with that and
mental pursuits and interests, but has learned to look
within, to discover his inner being, his spiritual self, to
aspire to overpass earth and her limitations. As he grows
more and more inward, his boundaries mental, vital,
spiritual begin to broaden, the bonds that held Life, Mind,
Soul to their first limitations loosen or snap, and man the
mental being begins to have a glimpse of a larger kingdom
of self and world closed to the first earth-life. No doubt, so
long as he lives mainly on his surface, he can only build a
sort of superstructure ideal and imaginative and ideative
upon the ground of his normal narrow existence. But if he
makes the inward movement which his own highest vision

has held up before him as his greatest spiritual necessity, then he will find there in his inner being a larger Consciousness, a larger Life. An action from within and an action from above can overcome the predominance of the material formula, diminish and finally put an end to the power of the Inconscience, reverse the order of the consciousness, substitute the Spirit for Matter as his conscious foundation of being and liberate its higher powers to their complete and characteristic expression in the life of the soul embodied in Nature.

SRI AUROBINDO

Our development takes place very largely by their [higher planes] superior but hidden action upon the earth-plane. All is contained in the inconscient or the subconscient, but in potentiality; it is the action from above that helps to compel an emergence. A continuance of that action is necessary to shape and determine the progression of the mental and vital forms which our evolution takes in material nature; for these progressive movements cannot find their full momentum or sufficiently develop their implications against the resistance of an inconscient or inert and ignorant material Nature except by a constant though occult resort to higher supraphysical forces of their own character. This resort, the action of this veiled alliance, takes place principally in our subliminal being and not on the surface: it is from there that the active power of our consciousness emerges, and all that it realises it sends back constantly into the subliminal being to be stored up, developed and re-emerge in stronger forms hereafter. This interaction of our larger hidden being and our surface personality is the main secret of the rapid development that operates in man once he has passed beyond the lower stages of Mind immersed in Matter.

SRI AUROBINDO

Supermind – Force of the New World

The Supermind is veiled here and does not work according to its characteristic law of being and self-knowledge, but without it nothing could reach its aim. A world governed by an ignorant mind would soon drift into a chaos; it could not in fact come into existence or remain in existence unless supported by the secret Omniscience of which it is the cover; a world governed by a blind inconscient force might repeat constantly the same mechanical workings but it would mean nothing and arrive nowhere. This could not be the cause of an evolution that creates life out of Matter, out of life mind, and a gradation of planes of Matter, Life and Mind culminating in the emergence of Supermind. The secret truth that emerges in Supermind has been there all the time, but now it manifests itself and the truth in things and the meaning of our existence.

SRI AUROBINDO

Supermind is the grade of existence beyond mind, life and Matter and, as mind, life and Matter have manifested on the earth, so too must Supermind in the inevitable course of things manifest in this world of Matter. In fact, a supermind is already here but it is involved, concealed behind this manifest mind, life and Matter and not yet acting overtly or in its own power: if it acts, it is through these inferior powers and modified by their characters and so not yet recognisable. It is only by the approach and arrival of the descending Supermind that it can be liberated upon earth and reveal itself in the action of our material, vital and mental parts so that these lower powers can become portions of a total divinised activity of our whole being: it is that that will bring to us a completely realised divinity or the divine life. It is indeed so that life and mind involved in Matter have realised themselves here; for only what is involved can evolve, otherwise there could be no emergence.

SRI AUROBINDO

... if supermind exists, if it descends, if it becomes the ruling principle, all that seems impossible to mind becomes not only possible but inevitable. If we look closely, we shall see that there is a straining of mind and life on their heights toward their own perfection, towards some divine fulfilment, towards their own absolute. That and not only something beyond and elsewhere is the true sign, the meaning of this constant evolution and the labour of continual birth and rebirth and the spiral ascent of Nature. But it is only by the descent of supermind and the fulfilment of mind and life by their self-exceeding that this secret intention in things, this hidden meaning of Spirit and Nature can become utterly overt and in its totality realisable. This is the evolutionary aspect and significance of supermind, but in truth it is an eternal principle existing

covertly even in the material universe, the secret sup-
porter of all creation, it is that which makes the emergence of consciousness possible and certain in an apparently inconscient world and compels a climb in Nature
towards a supreme spiritual Reality. It is, in fact, an
already and always existent plane of being, the nexus of
Spirit and Matter, holding in its truth and reality and
making certain the whole meaning and aim of the
universe.

SRI AUROBINDO

The descent of the supermind is a long process, or at least
a process with a long preparation, and one can only say
that the work is going on sometimes with a strong pressure
for completion, sometimes retarded by the things that rise
from below and have to be dealt with before further
progress can be made. The process is a spiritual evolutionary process, concentrated into a brief period; it could
be done otherwise (by what men would regard as a
miraculous intervention) only if the human mind were
more flexible and less attached to its ignorance than it is.
As we envisage it, it must manifest in a few first and then
spread, but it is not likely to overpower the earth in a
moment. It is not advisable to discuss too much what it
will do and how it will do it, because these are things the
supermind itself will fix, acting out of the Divine Truth in
it, and the mind must not try to fix for it grooves in which
it will run. Naturally, the release from subconscient
ignorance and from disease, duration of life at will, and a
change in the functionings of the body must be among the
ultimate elements of a supramental change; but the details

of these things must be left for the supramental Energy to work out according to the Truth of its own nature.

The descent of the supramental is an inevitable necessity in the logic of things and is therefore sure. It is because people do not understand what the supermind is or realise the significance of the emergence of consciousness in a world of inconscient Matter that they are unable to realise this inevitability. I suppose a matter-of-fact observer, if there had been one at the time of the unrelieved reign of inanimate Matter in the earth's beginning, would have criticised any promise of the emergence of life in a world of dead earth and rock and mineral as an absurdity and a chimera; so too, afterwards he would have repeated this mistake and regarded the emergence of thought and reason in an animal world as an absurdity and a chimera. It is the same now with the appearance of supermind in the stumbling mentality of this world of human consciousness and its reasoning ignorance.

SRI AUROBINDO

One thing seems obvious, humanity has reached a certain state of general tension – tension in effort, in action, even in daily life – with such an excessive hyperactivity, so widespread a trepidation, that mankind as a whole seems to have come to a point where it must either break through the resistance and emerge into a new consciousness or else fall back into an abyss of darkness and inertia.

This tension is so complete and so widespread that something obviously has to break. It cannot go on in this way. We may take it as a sure sign of the infusion into matter of a new principle of force, consciousness, power, which by its very pressure is producing this acute state. Outwardly, we could expect the old methods used by Nature when she wants to bring about an upheaval; but there is a new characteristic, which of course is only visible in an élite, but even this élite is fairly widespread – it is not localised at one point, at one place in the world; we find traces of it in all countries, all over the world: the will to find a new, higher, progressive solution, an effort to rise towards a vaster, more comprehensive perfection.

Certain ideas of a more general nature, of a wider, perhaps more "collective" kind, are being worked out and are acting in the world. And both things go together: a possibility of a greater and more total destruction, a reckless inventiveness which increases the possibility of catastrophe, a catastrophe which would be on a far greater scale than it has ever been; and, at the same time, the birth or rather the manifestation of much higher and more comprehensive ideas and acts of will which, when they are heard, will bring a wider, vaster, more complete, more perfect remedy than before.

This struggle, this conflict between the constructive forces of the ascending evolution of a more and more perfect and divine realisation, and the more and more destructive, powerfully destructive forces – forces that are mad beyond all control – is more and more obvious, marked, visible, and it is a kind of race or struggle as to which will reach the goal first. It would seem that all the adverse, anti-divine forces, the forces of the vital world, have descended on the earth, are making use of it as their field of action, and that at the same time a new, higher, more powerful spiritual force has also descended on earth to bring it a new life. This makes the struggle more acute, more violent, more visible, but it seems also more definitive, and that is why we can hope to reach an early solution....

This opens up roads of realisation into the future, possibilities which are already foreseen, when an entire part of humanity, the one which has opened consciously or unconsciously to the new forces, is lifted up, as it were, into a higher, more harmonious, more perfect life.... Even if individual transformation is not always permissible or possible, there will be a kind of general uplifting, a harmonisation of the whole, which will make it possible for a new order, a new harmony to be established and for the anguish of the present disorder and struggle to disappear and be replaced by an order which will allow a harmonious functioning of the whole.

THE MOTHER

24th April 1956

The manifestation of the Supramental upon earth is no more a promise but a living fact, a reality.

It is at work here, and one day will come when the most blind, the most unconscious, even the most unwilling shall be obliged to recognise it.

THE MOTHER

... this material world as it actually, visibly is, is so powerful, so absolutely real for the ordinary consciousness, that it has engulfed, as it were, this supramental force and consciousness when it manifested, and a long preparation is necessary before its presence can be even glimpsed, felt, perceived in some way or other. And this is the work it is doing now.

How long it will take is difficult to foresee. It will depend a great deal on the goodwill and the receptivity of a certain number of people, for the individual always advances faster than the collectivity, and by its very nature, humanity is destined to manifest the Supermind before the rest of creation.

At the basis of this collaboration there is necessarily the will to change, no longer to be what one is, for things to be no longer what they are. There are several ways of reaching it, and all the methods are good when they succeed! One may be deeply disgusted with what exists and wish ardently to come out of all this and attain something else; one may – and this is a more positive way – one may feel within oneself the touch, the approach of something positively beautiful and true, and willingly drop all the rest so that nothing may burden the journey to this new beauty and truth.

What is indispensable in every case is the *ardent* will for progress, the willing and joyful renunciation of all that hampers the advance: to throw far away from oneself all that prevents one from going forward, and to set out into the unknown with the ardent faith that this is the truth of tomorrow, *inevitable*, which must necessarily come, which nothing, nobody, no bad will, even that of Nature, can prevent from becoming a reality – perhaps of a not too distant future – a reality which is being worked out now and which those who know how to change, how not to be weighed down by old habits, will *surely* have the good fortune not only to see but to realise.

People sleep, they forget, they take life easy – they forget, forget all the time.... But if we could remember... that we are at an exceptional hour, a *unique* time, that we have this immense good fortune, this invaluable privilege of being present at the birth of a new world, we could easily get rid of everything that impedes and hinders our progress.

So, the most important thing, it seems, is to remember this fact; even when one doesn't have the tangible experience, to have the certainty of it and faith in it; to remember always, to recall it constantly, to go to sleep with this idea, to wake up with this perception; to do all that one does with this great truth as the background, as a constant support, this great truth that we are witnessing the birth of a new world.

We can participate in it, we can become this new world. And truly, when one has such a marvellous opportunity, one should be ready to give up everything for its sake.

THE MOTHER

VII

SPIRITUAL FORCES OF HELP AND SUCCOUR

A prayer, a master act, a king idea
Can link man's strength to a transcendent Force.
Then miracle is made the common rule,
One mighty deed can change the course of things;
A lonely thought becomes omnipotent.

SRI AUROBINDO
Savitri, Book One, Canto Two

The earth you tread is a border screened from heaven,
The life you lead conceals the light you are.
Immortal Powers sweep flaming past your doors;
Far-off upon your tops the god-chant sounds
While to exceed yourselves thought's trumpets call,
Heard by a few, but fewer dare aspire,
The nympholepts of the ecstasy and the blaze.

SRI AUROBINDO
Savitri, Book Four, Canto Three

Yet can the mind of man receive God's light,
The force of man can be driven by God's force,
Then is he a miracle doing miracles.
For only so can he be Nature's King.

SRI AUROBINDO
Savitri, Book Six, Canto Two

SPIRITUAL FORCES OF HELP AND SUCCOUR

Existence of Spiritual Force

Even in ordinary non-spiritual things the action of invisible or subjective forces is open to doubt and discussion in which there could be no material certitude, while the spiritual force is invisible in itself and also invisible in its action. So it is idle to try to prove that such and such a result was the effect of spiritual force. Each must form his own idea about that, for if it is accepted, it cannot be as a result of proof and argument, but only as a result of experience, of faith or of that insight in the deeper heart or the deeper intelligence which looks behind appearances and sees what is behind them. The spiritual consciousness does not claim in that way, it can state the truth about itself but not fight for a personal acceptance. A general and impersonal truth about spiritual force is another matter, but I doubt whether the time has come for it or whether it could be understood by mere reasoning intelligence.

Sri Aurobindo

All the world, according to Science, is nothing but a play of Energy – a material Energy it used to be called, but it is now doubted whether Matter, scientifically speaking, exists except as a phenomenon of Energy. All the world, according to Vedanta, is a play of a power of a spiritual entity, the power of an original consciousness, whether it be Maya or Shakti, and the result an illusion or real. In the world so far as man is concerned we are aware only of mind-energy, life-energy, energy in Matter; but it is supposed that there is a spiritual energy or force also behind them from which they originate. All things, in either case, are the results of a Shakti, energy or force. There is no action without a Force or Energy doing the action and bringing about its consequence. Further, anything that has no Force in it is either something dead or something unreal or something inert and without consequence. If there is no such thing as spiritual consciousness, there can be no reality of yoga, and if there is no yoga-force, spiritual force, yoga shakti, then also there can be no effectivity in yoga. A yoga-consciousness or spiritual consciousness which has no power or force in it, may not be dead or unreal, but it is evidently something inert and without effect or consequence. Equally, a man who sets out to be a yogi or Guru and has no spiritual consciousness or no power in his spiritual conscisousness – a yoga-force or spiritual force – is making a false claim and is either a charlatan or a self-deluded imbecile; still more is he so if having no spiritual force he claims to have made a path others can follow. If yoga is a reality, if spirituality is anything better than a delusion, there must be such a thing as yoga-force or spiritual force.

It is evident that if spiritual force exists, it must be able to produce spiritual results – therefore there is no irrationality in the claim of those sadhaks who say that they feel the force of the Guru or the force of the Divine working in them and leading towards spiritual fulfilment and experience. Whether it is so or not in a particular case is a personal question, but the statement cannot be denounced as *per se* incredible and manifestly false, because such things cannot be. Further, if it be true that

spiritual force is the original one and the others are
derivative from it, then there is no irrationality in sup-
posing that spiritual force can produce mental results,
vital results, physical results. It may act through mental,
vital or physical energies and through the means which
these energies use, or it may act directly on mind, life or
Matter as the field of its own special and immediate
action. Either way is *prima facie* possible. In a case of cure
of illness, someone is ill for two days, weak, suffering
from pains and fever; he takes no medicine, but finally
asks for cure from his Guru; the next morning he rises
well, strong and energetic. He has at least some justification for thinking that a force has been used on him and put
into him and that it was a spiritual power that acted. But
in another case, medicines may be used, while at the same
time the invisible force may be called for to aid the
material means, for it is a known fact that medicines may
or may not succeed – there is no certitude. Here for the
reason of an outside observer (one who is neither the user
of the force nor the doctor nor the patient) it remains
uncertain whether the patient was cured by the medicines
only or by the spiritual force with the medicines as an
instrument. Either is possible, and it cannot be said that
because medicines were used, therefore the working of a
spiritual force is *per se* incredible and demonstrably false.
On the other hand, it is possible for the doctor to have felt
a force working in him and guiding him or he may see the
patient improving with a rapidity which, according to
medical science, is incredible. The patient may feel the
force working in himself bringing health, energy, rapid
cure. The user of the force may watch the results, see the
symptoms he works on diminishing, those he did not work

upon increasing till he does work on them and then immediately diminishing, the doctor working according to his unspoken suggestions, etc., etc., until the cure is done. (On the other hand, he may see forces working against the cure and conclude that the spiritual force has to be contented with a withdrawal or an imperfect success.) In all that the doctor, the patient or the user of force is justified in believing that the cure is at least partly or even fundamentally due to the spiritual force. Their experience is valid of course for themselves only, not for the outside rationalising observer. But the latter is not logically entitled to say that their experience is incredible and must be false.

Another point. It does not follow that a spiritual force must either succeed in all cases or, if it does not, that proves its non-existence. Of no force can that be said. The force of fire is to burn, but there are things it does not burn; under certain circumstances it does not burn even the feet of the man who walks barefoot on red-hot coals. That does not prove that fire cannot burn or that there is no such thing as force of fire, Agni Shakti.

I have no time to write more; it is not necessary either. My object was not to show that spiritual force must be believed in, but that the belief in it is not necessarily a delusion and that this belief can be rational as well as possible.

SRI AUROBINDO

The invisible Force producing tangible results both inward and outward is the whole meaning of the yogic conscious-ness. Your question about yoga bringing merely a feeling of Power without any result was really very strange. Who would be satisfied with such a meaningless hallucination and call it Power? If we had not had thousands of experiences showing that the Power within could alter the mind, develop its powers, add new ones, bring in new ranges of knowledge, master the vital movements, change the character, influence men and things, control the conditions and functionings of the body, work as a concrete dynamic Force on other forces, modify events, etc., etc., we would not speak of it as we do. Moreover, it is not only in its results but in its movements that the Force is tangible and concrete. When I speak of feeling Force or Power, I do not mean simply having a vague sense of it, but feeling it concretely and consequently being able to direct it, manipulate it, watch its movements, be conscious of its mass and intensity and in the same way of that of other, perhaps opposing forces; all these things are possible and usual by the development of yoga.

It is not, unless it is supramental Force, a Power that acts without conditions and limits. The conditions and limits under which yoga or sadhana has to be worked out are not arbitrary or capricious; they arise from the nature of things. These including the will, receptivity, assent, self-opening and surrender of the sadhak have to be respected by the yoga-force, unless it receives a sanction from the Supreme to override everything and get something done, but that sanction is sparingly given. It is only if the supramental Power came fully down, not merely sent its influences through the overmind, that things could be very radically directed towards that object – for then the sanction would not be rare. For the Law of the Truth would be at work, not constantly balanced by the law of the Ignorance.

Still the yoga-force is always tangible and concrete in the way I have described and has tangible results. But it is invisible – not like a blow given or the rush of a motor car knocking somebody down which the physical senses can at once perceive. How is the mere physical mind to know that it is there and working? By its results? But how can it know that the results were that of the yogic force and not of something else? One of two things it must be. Either it must allow the consciousness to go inside, to become aware of inner things, to believe in the experience of the invisible and the supraphysical, and then by experience, by the opening of new capacities, it becomes conscious of these forces and can see, follow and use their workings, just as the Scientist uses the unseen forces of Nature. Or one must have faith and watch and open oneself and then it will begin to see how things happen, it will notice that when the Force was called in, there began after a time to be a result, then repetitions, more repetitions, more clear and tangible results, increasing frequency, increasing consistency of results, a feeling and awareness of the Force at work – until the experience becomes daily, regular, normal, complete. These are the two main methods, one internal, working from in outward, the other external, working from outside and calling the inner force out till it penetrates and is visible in the exterior consciousness. But neither can be done if one insists always on the extrovert attitude, the external concrete only and refuses to join to it the internal concrete – or if the physical mind at every step raises a dance of doubts which refuses to allow the nascent experience to develop.

Even the Scientist carrying on a new experiment would never succeed if he allowed his mind to behave in that way.

SRI AUROBINDO

Concrete? What do you mean by concrete? Spiritual force has its own concreteness; it can take a form (like a stream, for instance) of which one is aware and can send it quite concretly on whatever object one chooses.

This is a statement of fact about the power inherent in spiritual consciousness. But there is also such a thing as a willed use of any subtle force – it may be spiritual, mental or vital – to secure a particular result at some point in the world. Just as there are waves of unseen physical forces (cosmic waves etc.) or currents of electricity, so there are mind-waves, thought-currents, waves of emotion, – for example, anger, sorrow, etc., – which go out and affect others without their knowing whence they come or that they come at all, they only feel the result. One who has the occult or inner senses awake can feel them coming and invading him. Influences good or bad can propagate themselves in that way; that can happen without intention and naturally, but also a deliberate use can be made of them. There can also be a purposeful generation of force, spiritual or other. There can be too the use of the effective will or idea acting directly without the aid of any outward action, speech or other instrumentation which is not concrete in that sense, but is all the same effective. These things are not imaginations or delusions or humbug, but true phenomena.

SRI AUROBINDO

The fact that you don't feel a force does not prove that it is not there. The steam-engine does not feel a force moving it, but the force is there. A man is not a steam-engine? He is very little better, for he is conscious only of some bubbling on the surface which he calls 'himself' and is absolutely unconscious of all the subconscient, subliminal, superconscient forces moving him. (This is a fact which is being more and more established by modern psychology, though it has got hold only of the lower force and not the higher, – so you must not turn up your rational nose at it.) He twitters intellectually, foolishly about the surface results and attributes them all to his 'noble self', ignoring the fact that his noble self is hidden far away from his own view behind the veil of his dimly sparkling intellect and the reeking fog of his vital feelings, emotions, impulses, sensations and impressions. So your argument is utterly absurd and futile. Our aim is to bring the secret forces out and unwalled into the open, so that instead of getting some shadows or lightnings of themselves out through the veil or being wholly obstructed, they may pour down and flow in rivers. But to expect that all at once is a presumptuous demand which shows an impatient ignorance and inexperience. If they begin to trickle at first, that is enough to justify the faith in a future downpour. You admit that you once or twice felt a force coming down; it proves that the force was and is there and at work and it is only your sweating Herculean labour that prevents you feeling it. Also, it is the trickle that gives the assurance of the possibility of the downpour. One has only to go on and by one's patience deserve the downpour or else, without deserving, slide on until one gets it. In yoga the experience itself is a promise and foretaste but gets shut off till

the nature is ready for the fulfilment. This is a phenomenon familiar to every yogi when he looks back on his
past experience. Such were the brief visitations of Ananda
you had sometimes before. It does not matter if you have
not a leech-like tenacity – leeches are not the only type of
yogis. If you can stick anyhow or get stuck, that is
sufficient.

SRI AUROBINDO

In everyone, even at the very beginning, this spiritual
presence, this inner light is there.... In fact, it is everywhere. I have seen it many a time in certain animals. It is
like a shining point which is the basis of a certain control
and protection, something which, even in half-conscious-
ness, makes possible a certain harmony with the rest of
creation so that irreparable catastrophes may not be
constant and general. Without this presence the disorder
created by the violences and passions of the vital would be
so great that at any moment they could bring about a
general catastrophe, a sort of total destruction which
would prevent the progress of Nature. That presence, that
spiritual light – which could almost be called a spiritual
consciousness – is within each being and all things, and
because of it, in spite of all discordance, all passion, all
violence, there is a minimum of general harmony which
allows Nature's work to be accomplished.

And this presence becomes quite obvious in the human
being, even the most rudimentary. Even in the most
monstrous human being, in one who gives the impression
of being an incatnation of a devil or a monster, there is
something within exercising a sort of irresistible control-

even in the worst, some things are impossible. And without this presence, if the being were controlled exclusively by the adverse forces, the forces of the vital, this impossibility would not exist.

Each time a wave of these monstrous adverse forces sweeps over the earth, one feels that nothing can ever stop the disorder and horror from spreading, and always, at a certain time, unexpectedly and inexplicably a control intervenes, and the wave is arrested, the catastrophe is not total. And this is because of the Presence, the supreme Presence, in matter.

But only in a few exceptional beings and after a long, very long work of preparation extending over many, many lives does this Presence change into a conscious, independent, fully organised being, all-powerful master of his dwelling-place, conscious enough, powerful enough, to be able to control not only this dwelling but what surrounds it and in a field of radiation and action that is more and more extensive... and effective.

THE MOTHER

The Divine Grace

I should like to say something about the Divine Grace – for you seem to think it should be something like a Divine Reason acting upon lines not very different from those of human intelligence. But it is not that. Also it is not a universal Divine Compassion either, acting impartially on all who approach it and acceding to all prayers. It does not select the righteous and reject the sinner. The Divine Grace came to aid the persecutor (Saul of Tarsus), it came to St. Augustine the profligate, to Jagai and Madhai of infamous fame, to Bilwamangal and many others whose conversion might well scandalise the puritanism of the human moral intelligence; but it can come to the righteous also – curing them of their self-righteousness and leading to a purer consciousness beyond these things. It is a power that is superior to any rule, even to the Cosmic Law – for all spiritual seers have distinguished between the Law and Grace. Yet it is not indiscriminate – only it has a discrimination of its own which sees things and persons and the right times and seasons with another vision than that of the Mind or any other normal Power. A state of Grace is prepared in the individual often behind thick veils by means not calculable by the mind and when the state of Grace comes, then the Grace itself acts. There are these three powers: (1) The Cosmic Law, of Karma or what else; (2) the Divine Compassion acting on as many as it can reach through the nets of the Law and giving them their chance; (3) the Divine Grace which acts more incalculably but also more irresistibly than the others. The only question is whether there is something behind all the anomalies of life which can respond to the call and open itself with whatever difficulty till it is ready for the illumination of the Divine Grace – and that *something* must be not a mental and vital movement but an inner somewhat which can well be seen by the inner eye. If it is there and when it becomes active in front, then the Compassion can act, though the full action of the Grace may still wait attending the decisive decision or change; for this may be postponed to a future hour, because some portion or element of the being may still come between, something that is not yet ready to receive.

SRI AUROBINDO

Destiny in the rigid sense applies only to the outer being so long as it lives in the Ignorance. What we call destiny is only in fact the result of the present condition of the being and the nature and energies it has accumulated in the past acting on each other and determining the present attempts and their future results. But as soon as one enters the path of spiritual life, this old predetermined destiny begins to recede. There comes in a new factor, the Divine Grace, the help of a higher Divine Force other than the force of Karma, which can lift the sadhak beyond the present possibilities of his nature. One's spiritual destiny is then the divine election which ensures the future. The only doubt is about the vicissitudes of the path and the time to be taken by the passage.

SRI AUROBINDO

... when I speak of the Divine Will, I mean something different, – something that has descended here into an evolutionary world of Ignorance, standing at the back of things, pressing on the Darkness with its Light, leading things presently towards the best possible in the conditions of a world of Ignorance and leading it eventually towards a descent of a greater power of the Divine, which will be not an omnipotence held back and conditioned by the law of the world as it is, but in full action and therefore bringing the reign of light, peace, harmony, joy, love, beauty and Ananda, for these are the Divine Nature. The Divine Grace is there ready to act at every moment, but it manifests as one grows out of the Law of Ignorance into the Law of Light, and it is meant, not as an arbitrary caprice, however miraculous often its intervention, but as a help in that growth and a Light that leads and eventually delivers. If we take the facts of the world as they are and the facts of spiritual experience as a whole, neither of which can be denied or neglected, then I do not see what other Divine there can be. This Divine may lead us often through darkness, because the darkness is there in us and around us, but it is to the Light he is leading and not to anything else.

SRI AUROBINDO

... if one goes out of the determinism of the world as it is at present – this world which is a mixture of the physical, vital, mental and of something of a spiritual influence or infusion (quite veiled), everything that happens is the combination of all this – if we go out of all that (we can do it), if we rise above the physical, material world as it is, and enter another consciousness, we perceive things *totally* differently.

And then we see that behind these appearances which seem to us absolutely logical and extremely natural, and almost necessary, there is an action which, if perceived in one's ordinary consciousness, would seem *all the time* miraculous.

There is an intervention of forces, consciousnesses, movements, influences, which is invisible or imperceptible for our ordinary consciousness and *constantly* changes the whole course of circumstances.

We don't need to go very far; it is enough to take just a step outside the ordinary consciousness in order to realise this. I have already said several times that if one finds the psychic consciousness within oneself and identifies oneself with it, well, immediately one feels a complete reversal of circumstances and sees things almost totally differently from the way one ordinarily sees them. For one perceives the force which is acting instead of the result of this action.

At present you see only the result of the action of the forces, and this seems to you natural, logical. And it's only when something a little abnormal occurs – or it's a little abnormal for you – that you begin to feel surprised. But if you were in another state of consciousness, what seems abnormal to you now would no longer be so. You would see that it is the effect of something else, of another action than the one you perceive.

But even from the purely material point of view, you are used to certain things, they have been explained to you: for example, electric light, or that it is enough to press a button to start a car. You can explain it, you have been told why, and so it seems absolutely natural to you. But I had instances of people who did not know, who were completely ignorant, who came from a place where these things had not yet penetrated, and who were suddenly shown a statue being lighted up by rays of light; they fell on their knees in adoration: it was a divine manifestation.

And I have seen someone else who was in the same state, it was a child who knew nothing. In front of him a button was pressed and the car started; it seemed a *tremendous* miracle to him. Well, it is like that. You are used to certain things, they seem absolutely natural to you. If you were not used to them, you would see, you would think them miracles.

Well, turn over the problem. There is a heap of things you cannot explain to yourself, there is a host of interventions which change the course of circumstances and which you don't even notice. And so everything seems to you ordinary, monotonous and without any particular interest. But if you had the knowldge and could see that all these things which seem absolutely normal to you because you are used to them and have not even asked yourself "How does this happen in this way?" – if you had the knowledge and saw how it happens, what it is that acts, why for example someone who acts so imprudently that he would have broken his head does not break it, why everything seems arranged for a frightful accident to take place and it does not occur, and thousands, millions of things like that which happen every day and everywhere – if you had enough knowledge to see why it is like that, then at the same time you could say, "Look, there is something like a force, a consciousness, a power which acts and which is not from the material domain. Materially, logically, this is what should have happened, and it did not happen." You say, "Ah! it was his good luck", don't you? And then you are satisfied, it's all right for you.

(*Silence*)

It is the ignorant, limited, egoistic consciousness which demands miracles. As soon as one is enlightened, one knows that everywhere and always there is miracle.

And the more faith one has in this miracle and this Grace, the more capable one becomes of seeing it, or perceiving it constantly at every place where it is. It is ignorance and lack of faith, it is blind egoism which prevents one from seeing.

THE MOTHER

In the whole manifestation there is an infinite Grace constantly at work to bring the world out of the misery, the obscurity and the stupidity in which it lies. From all time this Grace has been at work, unremitting in its effort, and how many thousands of years were necessary for this world to awaken to the need for something greater, more true, more beautiful.

Everyone can gauge, from the resistance he meets in his own being, the tremendous resistance which the world opposes to the work of the Grace.

And it is only when one understands that *all* external things, all mental constructions, all material efforts are vain, futile, if they are not entirely consecrated to this Light and Force from above, to this Truth which is trying to express itself, that one is ready to make decisive progress. So the only truly effective attitude is a perfect, total, fervent giving of our being to That which is above us and which alone has the power to change everything.

THE MOTHER

VIII

LIFE – A MASS OF VIBRATIONS

Unseen here act dim huge world-energies
And only trickles and currents are our share.
Our mind lives far off from the authentic Light
Catching at little fragments of the Truth,
In a small corner of infinity,
Our lives are inlets of an ocean's force.

SRI AUROBINDO
Savitri, Book Two, Canto Five

LIFE – A MASS OF VIBRATIONS

For my consciousness the whole life upon earth, including the human life and all its mentality, is a mass of vibrations, mostly vibrations of falsehood, ignorance and disorder, in which are more and more at work vibrations of Truth and Harmony coming from the higher regions and pushing their way through the resistance.

THE MOTHER

"Chance can only be the opposite of order and harmony. There is only one true harmony and that is the supramental – the reign of Truth, the expression of the Divine Law. In the Supermind, therefore, chance has no place. But in the lower Nature, the supreme Truth is obscured: hence there is an absence of that divine unity of purpose and action which alone can constitute order. Lacking this unity, the domain of the lower Nature is governed by what we may call chance – that is to say, it is a field in which various conflicting forces intermix, having no single definite aim."

"Chance", Questions and Answers 1929-31

If chance is the expression of disorder in the lower worlds, still there are "happy" chances which are not necessarily the expression of a disorder, aren't there?

Happy for whom? For generally in this world as we see it, what is happy for one is unhappy for another; what is happy in one case is unhappy in another, and that too is an expression of disorder. I don't say that necessarily it is a chance occurrence which makes you unhappy, I say that it does not correspond to the order of truths, which is very different. One may be very happy in the midst of disorder! There are many who are perfectly satisfied with their disorder and would not like to change it.

> *A happy chance may come from a set of circum-*
> *stances which harm nobody.*

We do not see it harming anyone or anything simply because we do not have sufficient data. We cannot judge circumstances, for we do not know the world. What do we know about it? Our vision is so short and so limited. Just think, a man can never know what lies beyond his hundred and twenty years, at the maximum, and I am putting a very big limit, and I count the first years of his existence, though generally he does not remember what has happened then. What does one know about the world in so short a time? and about the consequences of things? Nothing at all. And even granting that one can remember sufficiently well to know the result or antecedent of a so-called "chance", it is altogether a local knowledge. What does one know about what is happening at the antipodes or in a million other places on the earth at the same moment? We know nothing about it. And as we know that all that happens is linked, that all things are closely linked, consciously, that there cannot be a vibration in one place without there being its consequences in another, how can we tell whether our chance is not harmful to someone, though it be favourable for us? I think it is impossible to form a judgment... how shall I put it? a correct judgment about things, for one does not know what is going on in the world. We do not know the whole, we know nothing of the play of forces. And we say that chance is the result of a play of forces; only, instead of being the expression of divine harmony, it is the expression of conflicting wills. These wills are not all necessarily bad or hostile but they are always ignorant. Each one tries to realise his own will and the victory is to the strongest – the strongest is not necessarily the best in this field. When one thing is realised, how many others could have been realised, which were not, because this one was realised? And all these things, we do not know.

THE MOTHER

Sweet Mother, I have not understood this: "At best we have only the poor relative freedom which by us is ignorantly called free will. But that is at bottom illusory, since it is the modes of Nature that express themselves through our personal will; it is force of Nature, grasping us, ungrasped by us that determines what we shall will or how we shall will it. Nature, not an independent ego, chooses what object we shall seek, whether by reasoned will or unreflecting impulse, at any moment of our existence."

The Synthesis of Yoga, p. 88

Not understood? What do you mean, "not understood"? It's a fact, there is nothing to understand, it's like that.

I have explained this to you I don't know how many times. You think it is you who decide: these are impulses coming from outside. You think you are conscious of your will: it is a consciousness which is not yours. And every-thing... you are made up entirely of something which is the forces of Nature expressing a higher Will of which you are unconscious.

Only, one doesn't understand this except when one can come out of one's ego, though it be only for a moment; for the ego – and this is its strength – is convinced that it alone decides. But if one looks attentively, one notices that it is moved by all sorts of things which are not itself.

But then what is mental and vital will?

That is an expression of something which is not personal.

If you analyse carefully, you see, for instance, that all that you think has been thought by others, that these are things which circulate and pass through you, but you have not produced this thought, you are not the originator of this thought. All your reactions come from atavism, from those who gave you birth and from the environment in which you have lived, from all the impressions which have accumulated in you and constituted something which seems to you yourself, yet which is not produced by you, but merely felt and experienced; you become aware of it in passing, but it is not you who created it, not you who gave it birth.

It could be said that these are like sounds – any kind of sounds: words, music, anything – recorded by an instru-ment, then reproduced by another instrument which plays them back like a gramophone, for instance. You wouldn't say that the gramophone has created the sound you hear, would you? That would never occur to you. But as you are under the illusion of your separate personality, these thoughts which cross your mind and find expression, these feelings which pass through your vital and find expression, you think, have come from you; but nothing comes from you. Where is the "you" which can create all that?

You must go deep, deep within, and find the eternal essence of your being to know the creative reality in yourself. And once you have found that, you will realise that it is one single thing, the same in all others, and so where is your separate personality? Nothing's left any longer.

Yes, these are recording and reproducing instruments, and there are always what might be called distortions – they may be distortions for the better, they may be distortions for the worse, they may be fairly great changes; the inner combinations are such that things are not reproduced exactly as they passed from one to the other because the instrument is very complex. But it is one and the same thing which is moved by a conscious will, quite independent of all personal wills.

When the Buddha wanted to make his disciples understand these things, he used to tell them: every time you send out a vibration, a desire for example, the desire for some particular thing, your desire starts circulating from one person to another, from one to another across the universe and will go right round and come back to you. And as it is not only one thing but a world of things, and as you are not the only transmitting centre – all individuals are transmitting centres – it is such a confusion that you lose your bearings in there. But these vibrations move about in a single, absolutely identical field; it is only the complication and interception of the vibrations which give you the impression of something independent or separate.

But there's nothing separate or independent; there is only *one* Substance, *one* Force, *one* Consciousness, *one* Will, which moves in countless ways of being.

And it is so complicated that one is no longer aware of it, but if one steps back and follows the movement, no matter which line of movement, one can see very clearly that the vibrations propagate themselves, one following another, one following another, one following another, and that in fact there is only one unity – unity of Substance, unity of Consciousness, unity of Will. And that is the only reality. Outwardly there is a kind of illusion: the illusion of separation and the illusion of difference.

Desires and all those things also?

This is not personal. Not at all personal. And that is *very* easy to find out; of all things this is the easiest to discern, because ninety times out of a hundred it comes to you from someone else or from a certain circumstance or a set of circumstances, or from a vibration coming from another person or several other people. It is very easy to discern, it is the first thing one can discern: it is a vibration which suddenly awakens something similar in you. You know, something makes an impact on you, and this impact brings up a response, as when you play a note. Well, this vibration of desire comes and strikes you in a certain way and you respond.

THE MOTHER

You must... understand that you are not separate individualities, that life is a constant exchange of forces, of consciousnesses, of vibrations, of movements of all kinds. It is as in a crowd, you see: when everyone pushes all go forward, and when all recede, everyone recedes. It is the same thing in the inner world, in your consciousness. There are all the time forces and influences acting and reacting upon you, it is like a gas in the atmosphere, and unless you are quite awake, these things enter into you, and it is only when they have gone well in and come out as if they came from you, that you become aware of them. How many times people meet those who are nervous, angry, in a bad mood, and themselves become nervous, angry, moody, just like that, without quite knowing why. Why is it that when you play against certain people you play very well, but when you play against others you cannot play? And those very quiet people, not at all wicked, who suddenly become furious when they are in a furious crowd! And no one knows who has started it: it is something that went past and swept off the consciousness. There are people who can let out vibrations like this and others respond without knowing why. Everything is like that, from the smallest to the biggest things.

To be individualised in a collectivity, one must be absolutely conscious of oneself. And of which self? – the Self which is above all intermixture, that is, what I call the Truth of your being. And as long as you are not conscious of the Truth of your being, you are moved by all kinds of things, without taking any note of it at all. Collective thought, collective suggestions are a formidable influence which act constantly on individual thought. And what is extraordinary is that one does not notice it. One believes that one thinks "like that", but in truth it is the collectivity which thinks "like that". The mass is always inferior to the individual. Take individuals with similar qualities, of similar categories, well, when they are alone these individuals are at least two degrees better than people of the same category in a crowd. There is a mixture of obscurities, a mixture of unconsciousness, and inevitably you slip into this unconsciousness. To escape this there is but one means: to become conscious of oneself, more and more conscious and more and more attentive.

Try this little exercise: at the beginning of the day, say: "I won't speak without thinking of what I say." You believe, don't you, that you think all that you say! It is not at all true, you will see that so many times the word you do not want to say is ready to come out, and that you are compelled to make a conscious effort to stop it from coming out.

I have known people who were very scrupulous about not telling lies, but all of a sudden, when together in a group, instead of speaking the truth they would spontaneously tell a lie; they did not have the intention of doing so, they did not think of it a minute before doing it, but it came "like that", Why? – because they were in the company of liars; there was an atmosphere of falsehood and they had quite simply caught the malady!

It is thus that gradually, slowly, with perseverance, first of all with great care and much attention, one becomes conscious, learns to know oneself and then to become master of oneself.

THE MOTHER

You live vitally in the vital world with all the currents of vital force entering, going out, joining and opposing each other, quarrelling and intermingling in your consciousness, and even if you have made a personal effort to purify your vital consciousness, to master in it the desire-being and the little human ego, you are constantly under a sort of obligation to absorb all the contrary vibrations which come from those with whom you live. One can't shut oneself up in an ivory tower, it is yet more difficult vitally than physically, and one takes in all sorts of things; and unless one is constantly wide awake, constantly on one's guard, and has quite an efficient control over all that enters, so as not to admit in one's consciousness unwanted elements, one catches the constant contagion of all desires, all the lower movements, all the small obscure reactions, all the unwanted vibrations which come to us from those around us.

THE MOTHER

... when we say that great waves of passion pass through people, and that they are not generated in them but pass through them, it is perfectly true. But if there was someone absolutely immune from all possibility of passion, they could pass by for centuries, he wouldn't even feel them. He could see them, see them passing, as one sees a storm passing in the sky, but he would feel nothing at all. When the vibrations inside oneself answer the vibrations from outside, it means that they are there; otherwise no vibration can enter.

There are examples like this. For instance, a crowd is seized by panic. Well, it is always possible that there are one or two persons who resist the panic, who are not touched, are outside it: they can save the situation. This has happened many a time. The reason why a movement, a vibration, a forceful movement is contagious is because the ground for contagion is there.

THE MOTHER

Does an individual mastery over desire suffice or is a general, collective mastery necessary?

Ah! there we are.... Is it possible to attain a total personal transformation without there being at least a correspondence in the collectivity?... This does not seem possible to me. There is such an interdependence between the individual and the collectivity that, unless one does what the ascetics have preached, that is, escapes from the world, goes out of it completely, leaves it where it is and runs away selfishly leaving all the work to others, unless one does that.... And even so I have my doubts. Is it possible to accomplish a total transformation of one's being so long as the collectivity has not reached at least a certain degree of transformation? I don't think so. Human nature remains what it is – one can attain a great change of consciousness, that yes, one can purify one's consciousness, but the total conquest, the material transformation depends definitely to a large extent, on a certain degree of progress in the collectivity. Buddha said with reason that as long as you have in you a vibration of desire, this vibration will spread in the world and all those who are ready to receive it will receive it. In the same way, if you have in you the least receptivity to a vibration of desire, you will be open to all the vibrations of desire which circulate constantly in the world.

THE MOTHER

It is only by a very persistent effort that one can succeed in overcoming his difficulties; and yet it seems impossible to cut oneself off completely from one's solidarity with the rest of the world. Therefore a perfect purity, a perfect perfection seem impossible so long as the world has not reached at least a certain degree of perfection. Even the ascetic, the solitary, who goes and sits in a cave or under a tree or in the jungle, cannot completely free himself from solidarity with the rest of the world. The air he breathes is full of all the vibrations of the world, the food he eats, whatever it may be, even if it is reduced to the minimum, contains the vibrations of the world; and so, it is enough for him to exist to be in solidarity with the difficulties of the world.

That is why, in fact, the way is so long. Even without having any other consideration than that of what one is absorbing constantly into himself when breathing or eating, all these things one must constantly transform as one goes on absorbing them. It is a continuous alchemy in which one absorbs a particular kind of vibration containing all the possible disorders and must transmute this into something which is ready to receive the light from above. And this work is perpetual, and perpetually renewed. So it is impossible to live in this world, in the world as it is, and become perfect without the world itself making a great progress.

THE MOTHER

GLOSSARY

*(The explanations of terms given below are based upon
Sri Aurobindo's writings.)*

Agni Shakti (*agni śakti*)
the force of fire.

Ananda (*ānanda*)
bliss, delight, beatitude, spiritual ecstasy; the essential principle of delight: a self-delight which is the very nature of the
transcendent and infinite existence.

Asura (*asura*)
the strong or mighty one, Titan; a hostile being.

Atma (*ātmā*); Atman (*ātman*)
see Spirit.

Body-consciousness
The body has its own consciousness and acts from it, even
without any mental will of our own or even against that will. A
great part of the body-consciousness is subconscient and the
body-consciousness and the subconscient are closely bound
together. The body-consciousness is only part of the whole
physical consciousness.

the Circumconscient
a secret environmental consciousness in which are determined
our unseen connections with the world outside us. It is
something that each man carries around him, outside his
body, even when he is not aware of it, – by which he is in touch
with others and with the universal forces.

Cosmic Self
the one Self inhabiting the universe.

daiva
    Fate, the influence of the Power or powers other than the human factor, other than the visible mechanism of Nature.

the Divine
    the Supreme Truth, the Supreme Being from whom all have come and in whom all are.

Dream Self
    The old Indian psychology divided consciousness into three provinces – waking state, dream-state and sleep-state – and spoke of the corresponding waking self, a dream-self, a sleep-self, all these three being regarded as derivations of the fourth, the supreme or absolute self of being.

the Force
    the power of Being in motion; the divine Force.

Hostile forces
    forces which try to pervert everything and are in revolt against the Divine and opposed to the Yoga.

the Ignorance
    a veil that separates the Mind, Body and Life from their source and reality, Sachchidananda; the consciousness of being in the successions of Time, divided in its knowledge by dwelling in the divisions of Space and the relations of circumstance, self-prisoned in the multiple working of the unity; it is called Ignorance because it has put behind it the Knowledge of unity and by that very fact is unable to know truly or completely either itself or the world, either the transcendent or the universal reality.

the Inconscience (Inconscient)
    In its cosmic manifestation the Supreme, being the Infinite

and not bound by any limitation, manifests in Itself, in its consciousness of innumerable possibilities, something that seems to be the opposite of itself, something in which there can be Darkness. Inconscience, Inertia, Insensibility, Disharmony and Disintegration; it is the Inconscient that is at the basis of the material world.

Karana (*kāraṇa*)
cause.

Karma (*karma*)
action; work; the principle of cause and effect in human life; accumulated seeds of past action.

the Life
see Life-force.

Life-force
the pure vital energy or life-energy, called Prana in Sanskrit.

mahātmā
a great soul.

Maya (*māyā*)
phenomenal consciousness; the power of self-illusion in *brahman*.

the Mental
see Mind.

Mind
In its ordinary use, the word covers indiscriminately the whole consciousness, but in the language of yoga the words "mind" and "mental" are used to connote specially the part of the nature which has to do with cognition and intelligence, with

ideas, with mental or thought perceptions, the reactions of thought to things, with the truly mental movements and formations, mental vision and will, etc., that are part of his intelligence.

Nature
the force or energy of Conscious Being which produces and moves everything in the universe.

Overmind
the highest of the planes below the supramental.

the Physical
outermost part of the being; everything has a physical part – there is a mental physical, a mind of the body; the emotional being has a physical part; the material is the most physical of the physical.

Physical mind
see the Physical.

Pisacha (*piśāca*)
demon; a (hostile) being of the lower vital.

Power
see Shakti.

Prakriti (*prakṛti*)
"working out"; Nature; Nature-Force.

prāṇa
the life-energy; life; the breath of life.

prāṇakoṣa
vital or nervous sheath; nervous body.

Psyche
  the soul; the essence of the soul; the spark of the Divine which
  is there in all things.

the Psychic
  psychic being; (sometimes) the psyche.

Psychic being
  the soul; when the psyche, a spark of the Divine which is
  present in all life and matter, begins to develop an individuality in the course of evolution, that psychic individuality is
  called the psychic being.

Psychic entity
  the spark of the Divine that descends into the evolution as a
  divine principle within it to support the evolution of the
  individual; it grows behind the mind, vital and physical as the
  psychic being.

Psychic personality
  see Soul-personality.

Purusha (*puruṣa*)
  Person; Conscious Being; Conscious-Soul; essential being
  supporting the play of *prakṛti*.

puruṣakāra
  "human effort"; energy of individual effort.

Rakshasa (*rākṣasa*)
  giant, giant power of darkness, a (hostile) being of the middle
  vital plane.

Sadhak (*sādhaka*)
  one who is engaged in the practice of *sādhanā* or yoga.

Shakti (*śakti*)
   Energy, Force, Strength, Will, Power; the self-existent, self-cognitive, self-effective Power of the Lord which expresses itself in the workings of Prakriti.

Sleep Self
   see Dream Self.

Soul-personality
   the psychic being or soul-form developing through evolution and passing from life to life.

Spirit
   the Consciousness above Mind, the Atman or Self, which is one with the Divine. The essential nature of our existence; the true being of the individual as well as the Self in the cosmos.

the Subconscient
   the part of the being which is below the level of mind and conscious life; in the average person, it includes the larger part of the vital being, the physical mind and the body-consciousness.

the subliminal
   comprises the inner being, taken in its entirety of inner mind, inner life, inner physical with the soul or psychic entity supporting them; (sometimes) all that lies outside the surface consciousness, including the subconscient, the subliminal proper and the superconscient.

the Superconscient
   consciousness above and beyond our present level of awareness in which are included the higher planes of mental being as well as the supramental and spiritual.

the Supermind
the full Truth-Consciousness of the Divine Nature in which there is no place for the principle of division and ignorance, and which is always a full light and knowledge superior to all mental substance or mental movement; in the supermind, mental divisions and oppositions cease, the problems created by our dividing and fragmenting mind disappear and Truth is seen as a luminous whole.

the Vital
the Life-nature made up of desires, sensations, feelings, passions, energies of action, will of desire, reactions of the desire-soul and of all the play of possessive and other related instincts, such as anger, fear, greed, lust, etc.

Vital plane/world
the world of sheer vital existence, ruled by desire and the satisfaction of impulse; the desire-world.

utkaṭa karma
"*karma* exceeding the usual measure"; certain strong effects of one's past actions that are unmodifiable.

Yoga (*yoga*)
a methodised effort towards self-perfection by the expression of the potentialities latent in the being and union of the human individual with the universal and transcendent existence.

Yogi/Yogin (*yogin*)
one who practises *yoga*; one who is established in realisation.

REFERENCES

The passages in this book have been culled from the following volumes
of Sri Aurobindo Birth Centenary Library and the Collected Works of
the Mother, published by the Sri Aurobindo Ashram, Pondicherry.

SRI AUROBINDO BIRTH CENTENARY LIBRARY

Volume	*Title*
9	The Future Poetry
13	Essays on the Gita
16	The Supramental Manifestation and Other Writings
17	The Hour of God
18	The Life Divine: Book One and Book Two, Part One
19	The Life Divine: Book Two, Part Two
20	The Synthesis of Yoga: Part One
22	Letters on Yoga: Part One
23	Letters on Yoga: Parts Two and Three
24	Letters on Yoga: Part Four

COLLECTED WORKS OF THE MOTHER

Volume	*Title*
3	Questions and Answers
4	Questions and Answers 1950-51
5	Questions and Answers 1953
6	Questions and Answers 1954
7	Questions and Answers 1955
8	Questions and Answers 1956
9	Questions and Answers 1957-58
13	Words of the Mother
15	Words of the Mother

All the extracts from the writings of Sri Aurobindo are in English;
those of the Mother are either in English or translated into English from
the French original.

The references below are given in an abbreviated form. A number set
in **boldface type** indicates the page number of this book on which a given
passage begins. The number which follows, if prefixed by SA, indicates

the volume number of Sri Aurobindo Birth Centenary Library; if prefixed by MO, it refers to the volume number of the Collected Works of the Mother. The subsequent numbers are the pages of the particular volume from which the passage has been extracted. For example, **3a.** SA22:478 means that the first passage on page 3 of this book is taken from volume 22 of Sri Aurobindo Birth Centenary Library, page 478.

The references follow:

3a. SA22:478 **3b.** SA22:477 **3c** SA18:329-30 **4.** SA22:393 **5.** SA22:479 **6a.** SA9:326 **6b.** MO5:306-07 **7.** SA22:470-71 **8a.** SA18:318 **8b.** MO3.60 **9.** SA22:477 **10a.** SA16:126 **10b.** SA16:127-28 **12.** SA16:157-58 **13.** SA22:467-68 **14.** SA17:258 **15.** SA19:809 **16a.** SA18:538 **16b.** SA22:478-79 **17.** SA23:841 **18a.** SA23:842 **18b.** SA23:841 **19a.** SA23:840 **19b.** SA23:840 **19c.** SA23:838 **20a.** SA13:211 **20b.** SA22:474-75 **21.** SA20:89-90 **23a.** SA13:566 **23b.** SA20:202-03 **24.** SA23:1079 **25.** SA23:578 **29a.** SA23:993-94 **29b.** SA18:555-57 **32.** SA22:358 **33a.** SA18:555 **33b.** SA20:170-72 **35.** SA22:353 **36.** SA22:356-57 **37.** MO6:366-69 **40.** MO4:260-61 **41.** SA18:426-27 **43a.** SA22:360 **43b.** SA24:1164-65 **43c.** SA19:891-95 **49.** SA22:288 **50.** MO7:222-23 **51:** MO5:394-95 **55a.** SA24:1573 **55b.** SA24:1572 **55c.** MO8:388-94 **62.** MO4:229-30 **64.** MO8:54-55 **66.** MO6:335-36 **67.** MO6:277-79 **71.** MO7:80-82 **72.** SA24:1570 **73.** SA24:1565 **74a.** SA24:1565-66 **74b.** SA24:1564 **75.** MO7:146-48 **78.** MO6:1 **81a.** SA23:1086 **81b.** SA23: 1087 **81c.** SA18:538-39 **82a.** SA18:543 **82b.** SA22:313-14 **83a.** SA23:1088 **83b.** SA23:1087 **84.** MO7:385-87 **86.** SA18:602-05 **90.** MO7:137-39 **93.** MO7:71-73 **96.** MO7:140-41 **101.** SA19:876-77 **102.** SA22:214-15 **103.** MO7:265-67 **106.** MO9:393-95 **108.** MO8:217-19 **111.** MO4:274-76 **114.** MO4:184-87 **117.** MO6:194-97 **120.** MO3:42-44 **123.** MO6:42 **124.** MO4:86-87 **125.** MO4:81-83 **127.** MO9:362-65 **135.** SA19:771-77 **140.** SA18:18-19 **141.** SA24:1499-1500 **142.** SA19:787-89 **144.** SA19:780-81 **146.** SA18:258 **147.** SA19:790-91 **148.** SA19:801-02 **149a.** SA16:73-74 **149b.** SA16:43 **150.** SA16:63-64 **151.** SA22:8-9 **152.** MO9:296-99 **154a.** MO15:104 **154b.** MO9:157-59 **159a.** SA22:221-22 **159b.** SA22:216-18 **162.** SA22:218-19 **165.** SA22:220 **166.** SA22:220-21 **167.** MO9:339-40 **168.** SA23:609-10 **170a.** SA22:475 **170b.** SA22:174 **171.** ˙MO7:382-84 **174.** MO9:420-21 **177a.** MO13:95 **177b.** MO4:406-07 **179.** MO8:51-53 **182.** MO4:35-37 **184.** MO4:335 **185.** MO6:430 **186.** MO4:382-83 **187.** MO6:446-47

INDEX